STOICISM

**How to Use Stoic Philosophy
to Find Inner Peace and Happiness**

BY JASON HEMLOCK

STOICISM: How to Use Stoic Philosophy
to Find Inner Peace and Happiness
by Jason Hemlock

ISBN: 979-8632761918

CONTENTS

INTRODUCTION

"It's time you realized that you have something in you more powerful and miraculous than the things that affect you and make you dance like a puppet."
—Marcus Aurelius

n an uncertain world, many of us are searching for something that will help us, if not make sense of it all, then at least be able to cope with the fast pace of change. Although our very modern lifestyle would be unfathomable to our ancestors, it's widely recognized that the ancient Greeks and Romans had figured out the answers to many universal issues we still deal with today. After all, although they might not be able to comprehend a world of iPhones and electric cars, problems such as relationship breakups, job loss, financial difficulties, etc. were just as prevalent then as they are now.

If you're looking to realise your potential and make the most of your experiences, there's a lot to be learned from ancient philosophers, who dedicated themselves to the question of what constitutes a good life and how you can make the most of your opportunities. There's a good reason why the ancient philosophies have stood the test of time and persist to exert an influence over us thousands of years later.

Stoicism is a type of Hellenistic philosophy that enjoyed a resurgence twenty or so years ago. It offers up a code of conduct and ethics, which empowers its adherents to live a good life. While Stoicism places an emphasis on self-discipline and improvement, an inevitable side effect of that process is that it empowers you to achieve your potential, enabling you to live your best life.

It is for that reason that Stoicism has proven popular among countless leaders, successful businesspeople and entrepreneurs, as well as famous musicians, artists and actors. It offers not just a roadmap to happiness, but guidance on how to achieve your goals, stay calm in challenging times and be your best possible, most authentic self.

You can sum up Stoicism with one simple idea: you need to accept full control of and take total responsibility for your thoughts and actions. When you do this, you step onto the path of personal fulfilment. Regardless of your social status, health or abilities, Stoicism will support you to become more than you ever dreamed possible, which is why it's proven to be so popular with successful entrepreneurs and leaders in their field.

However, as you'll discover when you follow a Stoic philosophy, Stoicism has a far greater potential than just self-help, as if that wasn't motivation enough to practice it.

When you take on a Stoic approach, you'll discover it has the potential to change the world around you permanently and for the good of all.

A brief overview of Stoicism

Stoicism was founded by Zeno of Citium sometime in the early 3rd century BC. He taught philosophy at the 'Stoa Poikile,' which is what gave the movement its name. Meaning 'Painted Porch,' the Stoa Poilike was a colonnade by the Agora in Athens, and in choosing the site, Zeno already demonstrated that what he was teaching was different to existing schools of thought, as most philosophers refused to teach in public places.

Taking a logical approach to personal ethics, Stoicism teaches that happiness comes from accepting each moment as it comes, an attitude somewhat akin to modern mindfulness, which is currently very popular. Stoicism states that an individual shouldn't allow themselves to be driven by either fear or a thirst for pleasure, but instead should seek to understand the world in which we live, find and fulfil your place in nature, and work in harmony with others, dealing with them in a fair and just manner.

Stoics held that external goals, such as health or wealth, are neither inherently good nor bad, but instead are there to act as a facilitation for virtue. This pursuit of virtue sometimes involved intentionally depriving yourself of the finer things in life, which is how this ancient philosophy came to give us the term 'stoic.' A stoic in the dictionary sense of the word is someone who is able to endure difficulties without complaint, and this is just one of the many benefits of following this philosophy.

As Epictetus says, "Don't seek for everything to happen as you wish it would, but rather wish that everything happens as it actually will—then your life will flow well." This attitude means that Stoics are especially well suited to cope with hardships and tough times, and are equipped with the mental fortitude to survive situations that might break another person.

However, it would be a mistake to believe that a Stoic doesn't feel emotion or care about pain. The Stoics sought freedom from being ruled by their passions by using logic and reason. They weren't looking to eliminate their emotions so much as transcend them by developing clarity of thought and inner peace. They looked to achieve a high degree of self-control, self-awareness and self-discipline.

Stoicism was – and is – an imminently practical philosophy. It is not enough to say the right things. To the Stoics, the best demonstration of one's beliefs came from their behaviour. If you follow the natural order of things, this includes bad as well as good times, and the ability to move with the flow of the tides is key to living a good life. If you are able to free your mind to think clearly and without bias, you will be able to understand the *logos* or divine reason flowing through the cosmos. In addition, you'll be able to rise above negative, petty emotions like anger or jealousy, giving you a healthier outlook on and experience of life.

Stoicism was highly popular across the Roman and Greek empires until the 3rd century AD. The Emperor Marcus Aurelius was one of its most quoted proponents. His *Meditations* is still considered to be an important philosophical text even today, and is a book you should read if you're serious about your Stoic studies. A prolific writer, he wrote many other Stoic letters and works during his lifetime, but sadly these have been lost in the mists of time.

As Christianity grew to become the state religion of Rome in the 4th century AD, Stoicism's popularity waned, but it has seen many resurgences over the centuries, particularly during the Renaissance and, of course, in modern times.

Famous Stoics

Following a Stoic approach to life has proven popular with highly successful people throughout the centuries. Many of the most famous names in history have turned to Stoicism to help them through their challenges, giving us very clear examples of how important Stoicism has been over the ages.

If you are wondering what Stoicism could do for you, here's a small selection of some of the most famous stoics throughout history to give you some inspiration:

Epictetus started his life as a slave. With the permission of his owner, he studied philosophy under the Stoic Musonius Rufus, and after he was freed, set up his own school. While none of his writings have survived, one of his pupils, the famous philosopher Arrian, transcribed Epictetus' Discourses and Enchiridion.

"If evil be spoken of you and it be true, correct yourself, if it be a lie, laugh at it."
—Epictetus

Seneca was a philosopher, dramatist and close adviser to Emperor Nero. Following a failed assassination plot, Nero ordered Seneca to commit suicide. Although Seneca was probably innocent, he was more concerned about comforting his loved ones than his own death.

"We should every night call ourselves to an account: what infirmity have I mastered today? what passions opposed? what temptation resisted? what virtue acquired? Our vices will abate of themselves if they be brought every day to the shrift."
—Seneca

Marcus Aurelius was the last of the Five Good Emperors and ruled over the Roman Empire from 161-180. His Meditations is a series of personal notes and letters, written to help him reflect on compassion, restraint, and self-humility. While it isn't likely they were ever meant to be published, Meditations has become one of the most influential Stoic texts.

> *"Time is a sort of river of passing events,*
> *and strong is its current; no sooner is a thing*
> *brought to sight than it is swept by and another takes*
> *its place, and this too will be swept away."*
> —Marcus Aurelius

Why you should be a stoic

So now you've had a brief overview of Stoicism and seen just how many high achievers follow a stoic philosophy, it should be obvious that Stoicism delivers results, not just in terms of unlocking your potential but in helping you achieve that all-so-elusive state of contentment.

But if you still needed a little more convincing to get involved yourself, here are a few more good reasons:

Stoicism gives you resilience in difficult times

Stoicism arose during a period when the world was in chaos. Just a few brief decades before, Alexander the Great had conquered the world then died in his early thirties.

His passing had a devastating effect on his Empire, plunging it into uncertainty.

Stoicism had a natural appeal during these troubled years because it gave followers a sense of security and offered a solid foundation during a time of conflict. Unlike religion, it didn't make any promises of a tranquil life after death, but instead focused on giving people a sense of calm during this one.

Because you never know what might happen, Stoicism contains an important lesson on not relying on anything that is subject to change. Your bank balance will fluctuate. Friendships come and go. Even the healthiest of relationships can end. Throughout all this change, the only thing with the potential to remain unaffected is ourselves. Every moment of every day, we make a choice as to how we react and respond to things. It is the only real power we have.

Although we have an innate instinct to react to something that hurts us, the Stoic approach is to strive to remain indifferent to external forces and maintain happiness, regardless of life's ups and downs. While it can be a challenge to keep calm in the face of adversity, once you've mastered this skill, you experience a release from being ruled by emotion and conversely enjoy a greater control over your life.

This isn't to say a Stoic doesn't feel anything. It is natural to be upset when something bad happens, but rather, a Stoic appreciates that negative emotions have their place and only become a problem if we let them be.

Right now, we seem to be going through a particularly turbulent time in history with a great deal of political uncertainty, so it would make sense to turn to Stoicism to help us weather the storm.

As Seneca wrote, "We suffer more in imagination than in reality."

Stoicism teaches tolerance and acceptance of others

Ancient Graeco-Roman society was divided by nationality, religion and status. Stoicism was revolutionary in being possibly the first Western philosophy to teach that slave and emperor are alike when Epictetus wrote that we are all "a member of the great city of gods and men."

Given that happiness is to be found within, rather than through, external events, when we take this a step further, social divides appear arbitrary and unnecessary. While the Ancient Greeks and Romans kept slaves, the Stoics held that we should remember that we all live under the same sky and come from the same place. Everyone deserves respect, regardless of who or what they are.

Given how far-reaching the Roman Empire was, bringing together countless religions, races and societies, Stoicism was an ideal philosophy for a world society needing to live together in harmony. Given modern globalisation, Stoicism helps us appreciate and embrace all the different ways of being without attaching superiority or inferiority to any of them.

Stoicism is compatible with religion

If you have a religious background, you might wonder whether you can be Stoic and stay true to your religion. If this is the case, you'll be reassured to learn that many of the beliefs we associate with the main religions originated with Stoicism.

Don't believe me?

The concept of multiple facets of a single, unifying God? Stoic.

The importance of following your conscience? Stoic.

The idea of controlling our negative impulses rather than allowing them to rule us? Stoic.

There's so much we owe to the Stoics, yet despite the fact that they gave us many enduring, powerful principles, nowadays we're more likely to associate those ideas with religion rather than philosophy.

It's unsurprising that there's a big overlap between Stoicism and Christianity. After all, Stoicism was a major guiding force on Roman society for centuries during the time when Christianity was first established and was finding its way. In fact, many early Christian leaders followed Stoicism before they came to the Church, bringing its influence with them.

In the early days of the Church, religious thought *was* Stoic thought.

As Christianity grew and became a guiding principle in its own right, church leaders broke away from Stoicism to promote their own unique religion. But just as Christianity owes a great debt to pagan practices for many of its festivals, it also has Stoic philosophy to thank for some of its fundamental concepts.

Stoicism is built for leaders

If you aspire to be a leader of any stripe, whether in business, politics or any other field, Stoicism is the philosophy for you. It teaches you to pick yourself up after failure and guards against arrogance when things are going well.

If you aim to influence the world around you, which is part of the responsibility of a leader, Stoicism teaches you to control yourself first. After all, you are the only thing which you can ever have complete control over. If you attempt to dictate how things should be, you risk disappointment when you fail. But if you are able to control yourself and know the best course of action in any eventuality, everything else is a bonus.

While we all have to deal with change in our lives, leaders are in a particularly vulnerable position in terms of the amount of risk and uncertainty they face. A Stoic attitude can help you remain calm in the face of uncertainty and help you prioritise what needs your attention and what you can delegate or put off until later.

For example, Barack Obama has been quoted as saying that while he was President, he tried to cut down the number of decisions he had to make in a day, so he left it to others to choose his meals or his clothes. With so many important choices riding on his discernment, he wisely said, "You can't be going through the day distracted by trivia."

While Obama may not specifically describe himself as a Stoic, the notion that it is important to focus only on what's essential is Stoicism in its purest form.

The Stoics knew that you're more likely to fail than to succeed, and this is okay. They were fully aware that the human condition means we'll feel angry, nervous, jealous, and all manner of negative emotions when things don't go our way.

But they gave us an easy-to-follow way of coping with these inevitabilities – a roadmap, if you will – to help us traverse life's ups and downs.

It's easy to be philosophical when things are going well. It's when times get tough that we face a challenge in continuing to practise what we've been taught. Stoicism offers a very simple way of establishing healthy mental habits and attitudes, which will sustain you through whatever life throws your way.

In this book, you will learn about all of Stoicism's most important guiding principles, including why you should actively experience tough times, how you can transform obstacles into opportunities, how you can harness the power of journaling to improve your outlook, how to prepare for the worst, how the Stoics approached mindfulness and why your lack of control is a good thing.

Each chapter includes practical exercises you can get started with immediately, so you can quickly see the positive impact Stoicism can have on your life.

To quote Epictetus, how long are you going to wait before you demand the best for yourself?

CHAPTER ONE

SEEK OUT MISFORTUNE

"You don't develop courage by being happy in your relationships every day. You develop it by surviving difficult times and challenging adversity."
—Epicurus

O ne of the reasons why Stoicism is enjoying a resurgence is because it offers a simple approach to combating the stresses and complexities of modern life. We live in what is arguably the most stressful time in history. We are expected to do more than our ancestors ever did, while at the same time feeling disconnected from the people around us. For many, community is a thing of the past.

All the modern technologies we have access to were invented with the aim of making our lives easier. In many cases, that's exactly what they do, but just as they can help us, they also risk causing us harm. Are you glued to your mobile? Addicted to social media? Easily distracted by the latest Netflix series?

The problem with these technologies is that our culture of celebrity worship and emphasis on living the perfect life on social media means that many of us fall into the trap of believing self-promotion is more important than self-improvement. Instead of looking inside to think about how we can improve ourselves, we create a false front to show the world that we're not just meeting society's expectations – we're smashing through them.

With TV reality shows promising overnight fame and fortune to those lucky enough to appear on them, it's easy to think it's more important to be someone who is paid for being an over-the-top version of themselves rather than becoming the best possible version of themselves. When instant gratification takes too long, it's no wonder so many are opting for the allegedly easy route.

But is this really making us happy? After all, you wouldn't be reading this book if you were satisfied with your life the way it is.

Believe it or not, this isn't a new problem. The ancient Stoics realised that one of the biggest issues we have to deal with arises from our urge to want more than we already have. It doesn't seem to matter how many things we accumulate or how much money we earn; we're pushed to want more and more.

But what is the real driving force behind that urge? The desire for a better life. So why are we getting it so wrong?

In a highly consumerist, materialistic culture, it can be very hard to ignore the pressure to conform and buy the latest designer outfit or most up-to-date phone, but that pressure is one of the biggest reasons why we're so miserable. In contrast, the Stoics pursued a simpler life, one ruled by self-discipline, which meant resisting going along with what everyone else was doing.

One of the most fundamental abilities of a Stoic is resilience in the face of adversity. Many Stoic philosophers considered the question of why bad things happen to good people and came to the conclusion that difficult times were inevitable, so it was important to be able to develop coping mechanisms for when they came. Our biggest lessons come through overcoming life's challenges and, as Seneca says, "I judge you unfortunate because you have never lived through misfortune. You have passed through life without an opponent— no one can ever know what you are capable of, not even you."

Our challenges enable us to understand ourselves better and learn our limits, as well as our potential. Seneca discusses this in great depth in his work, *On Providence*. He states that it is "not what you endure, but how you endure [which] is important."

It is an interesting book with many fascinating philosophical arguments. He felt that, for a decent man, his "good fortune is not to need good fortune" because when you have achieved the inner harmony espoused by Stoicism, it does not matter what happens to you; you have the strength of spirit to withstand anything life can throw at you.

This being the case, it is important to become a 'good' man long before anything negative happens so you already have the moral fortitude to be able to cope with it. Not only will you be able to weather the storm, those tough times will strengthen you. To use Seneca's words to illustrate this point, "No tree becomes rooted and sturdy unless many a wind assails it… the fragile trees are those that have grown in a sunny valley."

Another Stoic philosopher, Musionius Rufus, asked, "Could we acquire courage by realising that things which seem terrible to most people are not to be feared but without practicing being fearless towards them?" After all, things are only labelled positive or negative because of our perception. When we shift our perception, we recognize the positive and negative in *all* things, and can cope with whatever comes our way.

Misfortune is therefore essential to a Stoic way of being. It is an important tool to build our virtue and helps us become better people. In fact, according to Seneca, "God hardens, reviews, and disciplines those whom he approves, whom he loves." In other words, bad things happen to good people because it helps them become even better.

Taking this concept to its logical conclusion, Seneca recommends spending a certain amount of time on a regular basis actively putting yourself through hardship. As one of Nero's advisers, Seneca was a wealthy man, so he felt it useful to experience poverty to give himself perspective and build character. He suggested cutting back on the food you eat and restricting yourself to a very basic diet; wearing worn, old clothing; leaving your comfortable home with its warm bed and spending time on the streets. Now while we might not go to such extremes, when you put yourself in a position where you have very little, you remove its ability to frighten you. You experience the worst so it no longer holds any power over you.

So even if you don't deprive yourself of a place to sleep, it is important to actively seek out misfortune. This is not a philosophical exercise where you sit for a while and meditate on all the bad things that might happen. You need to actively live a misfortunate life so you do not fear it. We can become trapped in jobs that make us unhappy, stress about losing our beautiful home, or fail to appreciate what we have because we're too worried about what might happen if we didn't have it.

Stoicism tells us to be practical about this. Rather than anticipating what if, actively embrace misfortune. Create it for yourself, so if the worst ever happens, it's nothing new and doesn't destroy your life. After all, when we feel anxious or worried, this is usually more to do with a fear of the unknown than any actual experience. Yet we can become consumed by these negative states to the point where we are incapable of doing anything to assuage them.

So when you literally confront your fears, not only do you release their hold over you, you can also come up with ways to deal with them. Even if you've hit rock bottom, life is unlikely to stay there for the rest of your life. Almost everything we experience will pass.

For many of us, the thought of being without our phones or social media is terrifying, which is why it's so important to drop out temporarily. Switch off your mobile for a few days. Deactivate your Facebook account for a couple of weeks. What happens?

Life goes on.

It's a very easy way of introducing yourself to living a Stoic life and experiencing a taste of what might happen if your phone were stolen or you lost access to the internet. You may be old enough to remember life before social media took over, or you may never have known a world without your mobile. Either way, stepping back for a while gives you an important reminder that there is more to life than maintaining a front for the benefit of the outside world.

One of the more insidious effects of being in constant contact with the world at large is that we have very little time that is ours alone. I'll touch upon this in more depth in a later chapter, but think about how easily we give away our time because of our need to be 'social.' Even when you've gone on holiday, you're usually still reachable by text or instant message. There's very little opportunity to simply sit with yourself and reflect on who you are and who you want to be. By switching off for a certain amount of time, you can get a taste of who you might like to be when you're not attempting to meet other people's expectations.

Disconnecting from modern technology also gives you the chance to appreciate how lucky you are to have the technology you do. Not everyone has access to the internet or a mobile phone. You are incredibly privileged to be able to connect with your loved ones at the touch of a button, so I'm not saying you should permanently dispense with your phone and social media; just put it into context.

That's the whole point of actively courting hardship and becoming more self-disciplined. It helps you understand how wealthy you truly are and question your priorities. Why do you even have a phone? Is it to stay connected with your loved ones or is it to send out a signal about your status?

The true misfortune lies in the erroneous belief that superficial things are important. When we fool ourselves into thinking that our money and property are the things that make us happy, we set ourselves up for a lifetime of disappointment because there's always something better, always someone wealthier.

When we step back and experience a more basic, simpler life, we can get a sense of who we truly are when we aren't living in accordance with others' expectations.

Practical Exercise

There are a number of different ways you can welcome misfortune into your life on a temporary basis. Whatever you decide to do, it should be something that truly scares you, makes you feel uncomfortable and pushes you out of your comfort zone. You need to experience something you would ordinarily never willingly do for this exercise to work.

Aim to practice misfortune on a monthly, weekly, or even daily basis, as appropriate. Here are a few simple suggestions for you to use as inspiration for how you'll court hardship and tough times.

❖ *Take cold showers.* Sometimes it's the simple things in life that matter the most, and there's nothing more luxuriating than a long, hot shower. If you love your showers, try switching off the hot water. It's a stark reminder that you should never take anything for granted, and you never know - you may well discover you find cold showers invigorating.

❖ *Keep your home at an uncomfortable temperature.* Modern air conditioning and heating means we never have to feel discomfort in our own home. You can use this to your (dis)advantage by adjusting the temperature. Turn it off in the winter, so you have to put on extra layers to keep warm or wrap yourself up in blankets. Make your house hotter in the summer so you can't cool down. Eliminating modern conveniences make it easier for you to cope should you suddenly find yourself in a situation where you don't have the luxuries many of us consider necessities.

❖ *Eat a highly restricted, bland diet.* Decide you're going to eat nothing but rice and beans or bread and cheese or noodles for a set amount of time (e.g., a week or a fortnight). While you don't want to eat so unhealthily for a prolonged period, depriving yourself of everything but the bare minimum will show you that it is possible survive on very little in dire straits.

❖ *Fast on a regular basis.* Taking the restricted diet a step further, try abstaining from food completely for 24 hours every month or so. As long as you drink plenty of water, a day without food will not do you any harm (but check with your doctor if you have any medical concerns).

❖ *Step outside of your comfort zone.* We all have things that fill us with dread. Perhaps you don't have children and the idea of spending time surrounded by toddlers makes you shudder; maybe you don't like public speaking and do everything you can to avoid giving presentations at work. Whatever makes you feel uncomfortable, you should push yourself to do it. Offer to babysit a friend's colicky baby. Go to Speaker's Corner and give a speech about Stoicism. Go to a theme park and ride the biggest rollercoaster. Sing at a karaoke event. Actively participate in whatever activity you can think of that would be your idea of hell. When you face your fears in this way, you discover there are no limits beyond those you place on yourself, and you're capable of anything you put your mind to. You may even discover you enjoy something you thought you'd hate.

❖ *Volunteer to help others less fortunate.* So many charities are short-handed, and volunteering gives you the opportunity to do something good in the world as well as put yourself in someone else's shoes. Try volunteering at a soup kitchen or food bank; work at an animal shelter and clean out the dirty bedding; go litter picking, etc. Whatever you choose, aim to make it something you will find uncomfortable rather than looking for something that matches your strengths. If it's something you would happily do anyway, it defeats the purpose of the exercise.

❖ *Do your own DIY or gardening.* You may not be particularly handy with power tools or enjoying weeding, but there may come a time when you are not in a position to hire someone to do these jobs for you. Making yourself do those tasks you'd normally outsource to someone else offers so many benefits. It forces you to do something you don't want to do, but it also makes you slow down and pay attention to the moment. Chances are you won't be as good at the job as a professional, so you'll need to take care to do the best possible job. However, at the end of it, the feeling of accomplishment from doing something you wouldn't normally do and the knowledge you're learning a new skill is such a positive experience – and it reinforces your under-standing of just how much you can do when you push yourself.

❖ *Buy your clothes from charity shops.* There are a number of reasons why this a good thing. Unwanted clothing is responsible for a lot of land-fill and much of it ends up there purely because the owner decided they didn't want to wear it any-more. Buying second-hand clothes is an environ-mentally conscious way of shopping. However, this also serves the stoic purpose of courting misfortune because charity shops aren't necessarily up to date with the latest fashion. The choice is a lot more limited and restricted than in standard high street shops, although it should also be kept in mind that it's perfectly possible to find unworn or designer items in a charity shop, so in trying to be unfortu-nate, you may actually be fortunate!

❖ *Limit the amount of money you have to spend.* If you go out regularly, you may not be thinking about how much you spend on a night out. Try taking only a small amount of cash with you and once it's gone, don't get any more out. Take this a step further, and limit how much you spend in a given period, say, a month. Live as though you earned a lot less than you do and adjust your lifestyle accordingly.

These are just some suggestions. Feel free to think of ways that would be the most effective for you. Some of these may well be your normal way of living or things that aren't that big of a deal for you, so be creative and start living your worst life on a regular basis.

Summary

Actively seeking out misfortune will help you prepare for when things get tough.

- Take cold showers.
- Keep your home at an uncomfortable temperature
- Eat a restricted diet.
- Fast regularly.
- Step outside your comfort zone.
- Do volunteer work.
- Do your own DIY or gardening.
- Limit your cash spending.

CHAPTER TWO

TURN THE OBSTACLE UPSIDE DOWN

"We are more often frightened than hurt; and we suffer more in imagination than in reality."
—Seneca

One of the Stoic's approaches to dealing with challenges was to use a technique called Turning the Obstacle Upside Down. This is the concept that inspired Ryan Holiday's book, *The Obstacle Is the Way: The Timeless Art of Turning Trials into Triumph.* Just as with other Stoic ideas, it's a very practical approach that requires you to implement it and not just think about it.

As the name would suggest, the point of this attitude is to invert a problem to look for the silver lining in every cloud. If you look at it from the right perspective, every negative experience provides you with an opportunity for growth, or a teachable moment. As such, it should be welcomed and appreciated for the lessons it contains rather than feared.

Marcus Aurelius states, "The impediment to action advances action. What stands in the way becomes the way." So, if you lose your job, this gives you an opportunity to find a better job, change your career path completely or even take a break and spend time with your family. If you're dealing with a difficult colleague at work, this is not the universe trying to make your life hard. Instead, you're being given the chance to learn how to work with different personality types, develop patience or try doing things in a new way. If your relationship is going through a rough patch, this is your chance to take stock, reflect on how things are and see if there's anything you can do to improve things. This is your chance to consider how much you value your partner and whether they are the right person for you.

Ultimately, it doesn't matter what happens. The only thing you can control is your reaction to situations. The more you can free yourself from the erroneous belief that situations are inherently negative or positive, and instead view them as simply obstacles for you to navigate in the most effective way, the more you can grow as a person, develop resilience and move in harmony with the ebbs and flows of life.

If you examine the lives of successful leaders and entrepreneurs, there is a very clear common theme: they all grasp every single opportunity that comes to them with both hands, but more than that, they *create* their own opportunities. Examine the life of any leading light and you'll see that there were plenty of failures along the way. An overnight success only happens after years of preparation and setbacks.

When you follow a Stoic philosophy, whatever happens, there is always opportunity. So, while bad or unexpected things are bound to happen, you have the power to transform these into opportunity.

In fact, you will find it useful to move away from a mindset of 'good' and 'bad.' These terms are meaningless to a Stoic. Everything comes down to your perception, which is the one thing you have the ability to change.

So, for example, if you lose your job, you can decide to view it as the end of the world and sink into deep despondency, or you can see it as just another event in your life and look for the opportunities now open to you. Which of these is more likely to lead to employment?

There are three main processes involved in turning the obstacle upside down. These are perception, action and will. Each of these feed into the other and helps you shift your reality to where you want it to be.

Perception

Perception is how you interpret and react to what happens around and to you. Never underestimate the power of perception, because this is what shapes your life experience. Your perception is what makes you happy or sad. If you choose to focus your perception only on what makes you miserable, allow yourself to become emotional, or fail to take a long-term view before shaping your perception, you make your problems worse.

If you want to make the most of everything life has to offer, you need to learn how to limit the hold your emotions have over you. This can be a challenge, especially if you have fallen into the habit of expecting and looking for the worst, but if you can filter out your prejudices and expectations and view any given situation dispassionately and objectively, you'll see it as it truly is. This is a very powerful tool when dealing with an obstacle.

Practical Exercise

Make a list of the worst experiences of your life. Think about job losses, relationship breakups, financial difficulties, etc.

How did you deal with those situations at the time? What other possibilities were open to you? Were you aware of these at the time or did they only come to light later?

What happened as a result of your chosen reaction? How might that have been different if you'd taken an alternative action?

Where was the opportunity within that obstacle? Were you able to identify it?

Write down your answers to all of these questions and then take a moment to look at any recurrent themes. Where are your personal weaknesses? What do you need to work on?

For many people, they find that when something bad happens to them, they ultimately end up in a better place as a consequence. Is that true for you? If not, how can you make it true?

Now that you know you can turn any difficult situation into an opportunity, do you still view obstacles as negative? Or are they simply an event, neither good nor bad?

Action

Whatever happens to you, you take action by default. Even if you do nothing, this is still a form of action, so it is important you make the right choice moving forward.

While you have always taken action in your life, the real question is whether you have always taken the *right* action. In order to follow a Stoic path, it is important you take consciously directed action, which is driven by purpose in order to get you to where you need to be.

Having decided on the appropriate action, you can slowly begin to tackle your obstacles, moving forward step by step until they are eliminated. The right action involves having the bravery to act in your best interests from a long-term perspective, so, for example, if you are in a relationship that is not fulfilling you, you should have the courage to walk away and find the right person for you instead of staying where you are and remaining miserable for the sake of being in a relationship.

Taking Stoic action means you are no longer a passive slave to the world around you. Action is the only possible solution to whatever is troubling you.

Practical Exercise

Think about a current obstacle in your life. Make a list of all the possible actions available to you, no matter how silly, outrageous or seemingly impossible. Let your imagination run wild and don't allow yourself to be limited by excuses for why something might not work out.

For each of those actions, make a list of possible outcomes. Be as honest with these as you can and again, don't let emotion or negative thinking make you discount an option.

Now look at all these outcomes and decide which one best fits your ideal.

This is your way.

Will

When you 'will' something to happen, you are following your true path and going with the natural flow of things.

If you are genuinely following your will, nothing can stand in your way.

Your will is frequently confused with your 'want.' Often, people will believe that because they badly want something, it is therefore their purpose or destiny, but that is a misunderstanding of this particular principle. What's more, if you're pursuing something just because you want it, you open yourself up to disappointment when things don't go your way. You have fallen into the trap of being driven by desire rather than virtue.

Sometimes, all the action in the world still can't get you to where you need to be because of the surrounding circumstances. This is where your will comes into play; if the only available outcomes are all 'negative,' your will allows you to learn and grow from the experience, gain some humility and support others who subsequently go through what you're going through.

Your will helps you comprehend where you need to be rather than where you want to be.

In order to gain the resilience for tough times, we need to be able to accept whatever comes our way and seek out the lessons contained within.

Practical Exercise

Think about a time in your life when you wanted to do something, but obstacles were constantly thrown in your way.

What were the lessons you were meant to learn? Did you find a way to turn those obstacles upside down or did you take a different path? Did that different path lead to somewhere better? Or was it simply easier to give up? Did you feel like you were stuck in a particular place because the universe constantly slapped you back when you tried to break free? Do you really think the universe was stopping you or was there something else at play? Were you sabotaging your own efforts without realising?

If there is something you would like to do but haven't been able to for whatever reason, make a list of everything that is stopping you or might stop you.

Are those obstacles insurmountable?

There is very little in life that is truly impossible. As the saying goes, where there's a will, there's a way.

Decide on something you would like to achieve. List out all the obstacles you might face and then all the actions you can take to use them to your advantage. Recognise that the unexpected is always possible, but know that if it occurs, you have the will to navigate troubled waters.

Now make a commitment to yourself that you'll take the first step towards that goal, knowing that with each action, you progress a little closer until eventually you're where you want to be. In addition, you have the reassurance of knowing you have a Plan B because you've already prepared for the worst and are ready to deal with it.

Ultimately, life is a long series of challenges and problems. The real test is whether you are willing to let obstacles stop you or inspire you. Taking a Stoic approach means that not only will you have the confidence that comes from knowing you have the ability to deal with every problem; you *thrive* on them.

Summary

View obstacles as opportunities rather than road blocks. Use them to inspire you to action.

- Change your perception. Reflect on challenges you've dealt with in the past and what they taught you.
- Learn how to choose the right action. Think about a current problem you're dealing with and brainstorm potential solutions to help you pick the right path.
- Follow your will and go with the flow. Set yourself a goal to do something you've always wanted to do. Plan out how you'll get it done and take into account potential obstacles. Then put this plan into practice.

CHAPTER THREE

THIS TOO WILL PASS

*"Life is very short and anxious for those who forget
the past, neglect the present, and fear the future."*
—Seneca

T ake a moment to think about all the billions of people who've walked this earth over the entirety of humanity's existence. How much do we remember of them now? Within a couple of generations, almost all of us will be completely forgotten.

And even if we look at the tiny handful of people who've attained immortality through fame or infamy, how much do we really know about them? How much can we understand the complexity of their individual existence? We know about the important events in their lives, but do we know what their favourite food was? How they felt about their parents? Whether they were truly happy?

The point is, while some things matter, a lot of things don't, and by the time you leave this mortal coil, very little of your life will be left behind.

This could be incredibly depressing if viewed from a certain perspective, but, as we examined in the last chapter, as Stoics, we're working on shifting our perspective. The important point here is that in the grand scheme of things, no matter who you are, we're *all* very small and trivial.

Back in Roman times, they would celebrate every big military victory with a 'triumph.' This would involve a grand procession of generals so everyone could cheer their efforts. Festivities would last all day and possibly into the next as everyone gave thanks for their win.

But behind the generals would stand a slave, whose job it was to whisper, "Remember you are mortal." Victory is fleeting and no matter how high you rise, you can come crashing back down to earth at any time.

So, if nothing lasts forever, what's really important? This moment right now. The *only* thing that matters is being the best person you can be at all times.

For example, Alexander the Great had the biggest empire the world has ever known. His influence was so great, cities still bear his name to this day. Yet all his achievements paled into insignificance when he got drunk and fought with his close friend, Cleitus, accidentally killing him. Alexander fell into a deep depression and wouldn't eat or drink for days. What did all his achievements matter after the loss of a friend? Is it really a good thing to have cities named after you if you're hurting the ones you love?

If you are your best, most authentic self in every moment, it doesn't matter what else happens. Nothing can take that away from you. As Marcus Aurelius puts it, "Be like the rocky headland on which the waves constantly break. It stands firm, and round it the seething waters are laid to rest." The world can go crazy around you, but if you have an inward focus and strive to do the right thing, you will navigate the storm.

We experience life in the present, but most of the time we're living in the future or the past, letting the present slip away without conscious thought. We're counting down the days until we next go on holiday, but while we're on vacation, we're worried about how quickly our break will be over. We fret about past mistakes and things we've done wrong or stress about what might happen in the future. We flit from thought to thought, but fail to stop and appreciate what's happening right now.

As a Stoic, you should aspire to live in the moment as much as possible. In modern times, this is what many people call 'mindfulness.' Living in the moment involves maintaining an active focus on the present, sitting with your thoughts as they arise, letting them be as they will rather than inviting or repelling them. When you are able to do this, you are able to fully live your life instead of letting it pass you by.

Living in the present moment has a number of documented benefits. Studies have shown it lowers stress, boosts your immune system and lowers your blood pressure. It can even help people cope with chronic pain and cancer. What's more, it leads to greater self-awareness and is another tool to help you cope with negative situations and people.

By now, you should be convinced of the positive impact of being mindful of the present moment. However, while in theory this is easy, in practise it's very difficult. The problem is that as soon as you start trying to live in the now because you want to enjoy the benefits, you make it impossible to embrace the present because knowing you'll receive something good from it puts your focus on the future, which undermines everything you want to do.

It's quite a Catch 22!

Switching your focus so you're genuinely living in the now takes determination, intention and active practice. You need to let go of the outcome and simply enjoy the process.

Practical Exercises

There are a number of different ways you can bring yourself into the present and stay there. Start with one or two from these suggestions and build upon them. You might find some work better for you than others, which is fine – this is an individual journey with many different routes to success.

❖ *Forget yourself.* Have you ever danced like no one's watching? Let your body move without caring what it looks like? Did you notice that it was much easier to perform a particular movement when you weren't actively thinking about it?

As soon as you start thinking about being mindful, you lose the magic of the moment. You need to forget about what you're trying to do and just do it. The more you concentrate on why you can't be mindful and strive to achieve that state, the more impossible it becomes. Instead, forget about your thoughts or fear of failure, and see more of what's going on around you.

See yourself as part of the current moment rather than separate from it. Immerse yourself in your current experience.

At random moments during the day, pause and examine what's going on around you. What can you see? What can you smell? What can you hear?

Take it a step further. Close your eyes and notice the little sounds you normally filter out. Maybe it's the background buzz of traffic. Perhaps you can hear birdsong if you concentrate.

Open your eyes and look around you. See your surroundings with new eyes. And then breathe.

Inhale deeply three times and savour this unique moment in time, knowing it will never be exactly like this again.

❖ *Don't let the future or past spoil your enjoyment of the present.* Frequently, we get so caught up in thinking about what has happened or what might have happened, we can't fully appreciate what's happening in the present. Maybe you've been on holiday and thought 'this is the kind of lifestyle to which I want to become accustomed' without recognising this is *already* your lifestyle. Or you go to a restaurant and think the food wasn't as good as the last time you came.

Choose a mundane activity, something you do every day, and slow it right down. It might be your morning cup of coffee or your walk to get lunch. Whatever you choose, take the time to actively consider every single second. *Feel* it with every single sense and appreciate the beauty of the fact you're here to have that experience.

When your attention is solely on what is happening right now, it's impossible to worry about the past or future. This is how you can transform the mundane into a meditative experience.

❖ *Forget about time.* Can you think of a time when you were so caught up in what you were doing, you lost track of time? This is a state known as being in the flow.

On the surface of it, this concept contains a paradox. If you aren't aware of the current moment, how can you be living in it? But the point about flow is that you're so deeply focused on what's currently happening, it's impossible to notice anything else, including time. This is why time flies when you're having fun.

When you're in the flow, it's impossible to maintain it as soon as you become aware of it. And it's difficult to achieve intentionally because that runs counter to the nature of flow. All you can do is put yourself in a position where you're likely to enter that state and let it happen as it will.

How can you create the right conditions? First, give yourself a goal that will challenge you but is achievable. It needs to be easy enough you won't get frustrated, but not so easy you'll get bored. Then break it down into tiny little steps, so you know exactly where you're going. It might be doing another length in the pool, colouring another section of a picture or turning the page to read what happens next in your novel. You're anticipating what's coming while at the same time appreciating what's happening right now.

When you get into the flow, you lose all awareness of your surroundings and your world becomes nothing but yourself and your activity. You feel a continual sense of control over your current situation and you're getting a positive feeling from your activity, so you're working without feeling like you're making any real effort.

❖ *Stay in the zone.* We've all had those times of suddenly 'waking up' to realise we have absolutely no idea what's been happening over the past few minutes and have been working on autopilot. This is the very opposite of mindfulness – instead, you're being mind*less* because you're so caught up in your thoughts, you don't notice anything around you.

This happens because you cease paying attention to things you think you know inside out. This is why you frequently zone out during your commute – you've done the journey so many times before, you think you know every aspect of it so it has nothing new to offer. Yet if you examine the world around you as if you've never seen it before, you'll quickly discover that everything changes all the time. As the saying goes, you can never step in the same river twice because it's never the same river and you're never the same person. The way the light falls, the expression on someone's face, how you're feeling that morning – all of these things change and make each experience brand new.

Notice six new things about your environment every day. Actively seek out things you haven't noticed or look for how things have subtly changed since yesterday. Not only will this help you be more mindful, it also demonstrates very obviously how nothing ever stays the same.

❖ *Breathe.* This is one of the simplest ways to be mindful. If you feel yourself losing grasp on the present, simply become aware of your breath. When you do this, you automatically bring yourself into the present. It's always with you and always happening *now.*

So if all else fails, just breathe.

Summary

All we truly possess is the current moment, so make every moment count.

- Stay in the magic of the moment.
- Don't let the future or the past ruin your experience of the present.
- Forget about time.
- Stay in the zone.
- Breathe.

CHAPTER FOUR

VIEW THE WORLD FROM ABOVE

"If anyone can refute me – show me I'm making a mistake or looking at things from the wrong perspective – I'll gladly change. It's the truth I'm after, and the truth never harmed anyone."
—Marcus Aurelius

Marcus Aurelius was very fond of following a practise called 'taking the view from above.' Also dubbed 'Plato's view,' this exercise involves stepping away from our lives and viewing it from a broader perspective. This goes beyond simply looking objectively at your problems, but seeing yourself as just one of billions of people, everyone all around the globe living their lives and dealing with their own issues.

Taking this approach reminds you of just how small you are in the grand scheme of things. Recognising that very few things are worth worrying about helps you put your current issues into perspective and see that stressing about them is a waste of energy.

However, this is just the first step in achieving Plato's view. If you want to get the most out of this technique, you need to go deeper and access what the Stoics termed 'sympatheia.' This is where you see yourself as having a mutual co-dependence with all of humanity. If you were able to go out in space and enjoy a literal view from above, you'd be able to see that we're all the same, no matter what our station in life, and that there is a lot we can all do to make the world a better place.

When you achieve Plato's view, you transcend your own concerns and remember your duty to those around you, both friends and strangers. Shifting your focus from your individual needs to that of the whole of humanity has the potential to make you massively change the way you see the world around you. The Stoics believed this would give you inner peace, as it would eliminate anger or pain, filling you instead with love and compassion, even for those who hurt us.

Looking at things from this angle, all people are equal, with no one life having more value than another, regardless of status. As Aurelius puts it, "Think of substance in its entirety, of which you have the smallest of shares; and of time in its entirety, of which a brief and momentary span has been assigned to you; and of the works of destiny, and how very small is your part in them."

Aurelius goes on to discuss that even for those who have achieved great fame, the second they die, they are no longer relevant. He goes on to say that even for those who are remembered for their deeds, this is "sheer vanity and nothing more."

Harsh words, but when you look into the underlying philosophy, what remains when you strip all your achievements away? The importance of living a good life, striving to always do what is right for the common good, and accepting whatever comes your way because every experience is a lesson. Further, while it may be that nothing of us survives after we're gone, when you see everything from an eternal viewpoint, there is beauty all around us, even at the moment of decay. That beauty comes from the fact that nothing lasts forever, so our own mortality is a beautiful thing. Aurelius argued that our lack of personal significance is irrelevant because we are all part of the cosmos, which is in itself inherently beautiful.

When you see yourself as a tiny speck in the eternity of the cosmos, everything is trivial. Nothing is important. Yet at the same time, everything we do matters, because we are all contributing to something far greater than ourselves.

Life is a gift all on its own. Anything else is a bonus.

Practical Exercise

We all know that meditation is good for us, but many people struggle to develop this practice. Regular meditation can combat stress, help you develop mental clarity and support your Stoic work.

Guided meditations are a great way to get into meditation if you've been struggling to meditate regularly. They don't require regular practice, so you can just do them as and when you feel the need.

This meditation is designed to give you Plato's view. You can try to memorise it and replay it in your mind, but you might find it more effective to record it in advance and play it so you can simply relax and enjoy the meditation.

Do not meditate lying down – you're likely to fall asleep! Instead, either sit cross-legged on a cushion against the wall, or on a chair that supports your back so you stay upright, alert and comfortable during your meditation.

Have some food ready to eat after the meditation is done so you can ground yourself.

Meditation to give you Plato's view

Sit comfortably and just take a moment to focus on your breath. Notice as you inhale and exhale... inhale and exhale...

Now as you inhale, imagine you are breathing in a beautiful, calming white light. And as you exhale, release any negativity or stress you may have been holding on to.

Continue to breathe in that beautiful white light. Feel it filling your body with peaceful energy, making you feel lighter... and lighter... and lighter...

And as your body continues to get lighter and lighter, feel yourself starting to float out of your body. You are completely safe as you hover above your body and look down on yourself.

Passively observe yourself sitting there. Notice how you look relaxed and calm and know your body is perfectly safe as you start to float higher and higher.

Now you are outside, hovering above the building your body is in. Look down upon it and see what it looks like from above. Examine the surrounding area – are there gardens? Streets? Cars? Are there people walking around?

Look carefully at the area. Notice all the little details. Think about the people in any buildings you can see going about their business, each of them having their own concerns and worries.

Now rise higher and higher until you are at cloud level. Look down beneath you. See the land stretching out as far as you can see. Notice the curve of the horizon off in the distance.

Feel yourself at peace, knowing you are safe so high in the sky. The world below you seems so small and insignificant, but your journey is not yet done.

You feel yourself going higher again, up, up and out of the atmosphere and into space. You are perfectly safe as you float out towards the moon. Looking back at the earth, it looks like a small ball below you. From this distance, all you can see are the clouds swirling around, the green of the land, the blue of the ocean.

Billions of souls are going about their lives but from this distance, they may as well be dust.

You feel yourself travelling farther and farther away from the earth until you find yourself deep in the heart of the cosmos. All around you are stars, twinkling in a stunning display of natural beauty.

Take a moment to breathe in the wonder around you. Appreciate that everything is as it should be, your life unfolding exactly how it needs to. See the countless stars and know that there are countless more out of sight.

Appreciate that the cosmos is infinite and you are infinitesimal.

When you are ready, take one last deep breath, inhaling the essence of the cosmos, then tell yourself it is time to return to your body.

You find yourself immediately back in your body, sitting where you started. Take a moment to focus on your breath, inhaling and exhaling as you ground yourself fully into yourself.

When you are ready, open your eyes and see the world around you anew.

Summary

Step back to take Plato's view to give yourself perspective.

- Do the Plato's view meditation.

CHAPTER FIVE

MEMENTO MORI

*"Think of the life you have lived until now as over
and, as a dead man, see what's left as a bonus and live it
according to Nature. Love the hand that fate deals you
and play it as your own, for what could be more fitting?"*
—Marcus Aurelius

The concept of *Memento Mori* involves reflecting on your own mortality. This ancient practice actually predates Stoicism – it was Socrates who first stated that the purpose of philosophy was to consider "dying and being dead." The Stoics took this very important lesson and used it as inspiration. After all, you could die at any moment, so you should use that to inform everything you do, say and think. You shouldn't wait to live a life of virtue – there is no time like the present to follow a virtuous life because you may not have a future.

While you might think that considering your death might be depressing, that's only the case if you miss the point. To a Stoic, the thought of death is inspirational as well as humbling. Seneca advised to think 'you may not wake up tomorrow' when you go to bed and then 'you may not sleep again' when you wake up the next day.

Constantly reminding yourself that life is short so you should make the most of whatever time you have left should be a motivation to be your very best self all the time. This can be difficult to maintain, as death is one of the few taboos remaining in Western culture. Many of us are afraid to even consider it, let alone regularly meditate on it. From a Stoic perspective, however, if you have striven to live a meaningful life, there is nothing to be afraid of. Death comes to us all. It's a part of the natural cycle of life, so you cannot escape it. Doesn't it make sense to prepare for it by giving your life purpose?

Now it is easy to get caught up in fantasies when you start thinking about what you would do if this were your last day alive. If you knew you only had 24 hours to live, the chances are high you'd do all sorts of outrageous things, like stay off work, do something fun with your family and friends, and maybe even break a few laws because there's no chance of punishment.

This isn't exactly a sustainable way of leaving, and it's certainly not what the Stoics intended when they taught the practice of *Memento Mori*. Instead, you should be thinking about how you would feel if you died unexpectedly. Had you practised kindness? Had you worked as hard as you could? Did you attempt to be your best self at all times? In short, if you left this earth now, would you be happy with your legacy?

When you consider death from this perspective, it shouldn't be depressing or fearful. Instead, it should drive you towards making the most of every single day. Did you spend enough time with your children or did you play silly games on your phone instead? Did you binge watch Netflix instead of phoning your parents? In short, was this the best possible day you could have had, even if it was completely ordinary?

Practical Exercises

✓ *Read biographies and autobiographies about death and dying.* One of the best ways to demystify and remove the stigma around death is to immerse yourself in it. Reading memoirs on the subject can help you see how others have approached it and what they have learned through their experiences. Look at the biography section of bookshops, libraries or Amazon for any that appeal to you, or if you need a few suggestions to get you started, you could try *Nothing to be Frightened of* by Julian Barnes, *When Breath Becomes Air* by Paul Kalanithi, *The Year of Magical Thinking* by Joan Didion, *The Bright Hour: A Memoir of Living and Dying* by

Nina Riggs, *The End of your Life Book Club* by Will Schwalbe, or *Dying: A Memoir* by Cory Taylor.

✓ *Plan your funeral and write your own eulogy.* Planning your own funeral is a good idea, regardless of whether you're a Stoic or not. Not only is it surprisingly good fun, there's a lot to be said for making it easy for your loved ones to know what to do when the time comes to say goodbye. While funerals are for the living, knowing that it reflects exactly what you wanted gives a lot of reassurance to those you leave behind and gives them one final reminder of who you were.

When it comes to writing your eulogy, be honest about yourself. While those you leave behind will feel obligated to talk about the positive, you are under no such obligation. Will your children say you made time for them? Will your partner say you were thoughtful and loving? Will those who knew you say you always did your best to live a good life?

Or will they wish you had done more to be a better person?

It is okay if you realize you could have tried harder. It's never too late to change. So revisit your eulogy on a regular basis and reflect on what kind of legacy you're currently leaving behind and how you can change things so your eulogy reflects what you would want it to say.

✓ *At the end of every day, take a moment to look back and reflect.* Journaling is becoming increasingly popular because it helps us take stock of where we are and where we would like to be. Take ten minutes each evening to answer these simple questions:

- If you don't wake up in the morning, would you be happy that this was your last day?
- What would you do differently if you could go back in time?
- Would you change how you interacted with people?
- How will you use this reflection to have a better day tomorrow?
- Did you meet your goals?

Set a small number of actionable goals for tomorrow that will help you have a better day and help you work towards a more virtuous life, whatever virtuous means to you. Remember – Stoicism is a practical philosophy, so this will help you bring it into your daily life.

✓ *Meditate on your mortality. Literally.* We've already discussed the benefits of meditation. You can use this ancient practice to help you accept the inevitability of death, and support you in living your best life. Again, you may want to record this script and play it back to help you focus while you meditate. If you do that, leave some time where appropriate for you to reflect on the questions.

Meditation on death

Sit down and make yourself comfortable, ensuring your back is supported.

Take a moment to focus on your breath. Observe it as you inhale and exhale... Inhale and exhale...

And as you inhale, feel that breath filling you with warming energy, helping you relax.

And as you exhale, breathe out any negativity, any stress, any worry.

Continue to inhale that warming energy and exhale any negativity.

Now, as you inhale, feel yourself sinking down... down... down... Going deep into the earth.

You feel perfectly safe. Nothing can harm you here.

You find yourself standing on the edge of a river. Ahead of you is a small boat, a tall, silent figure dressed in black waiting patiently in the boat for you.

He holds out a hand and beckons you to join him on board.

You realise this is the River Styx and this is the ferryman, come to take you to the afterlife.

Once you cross this river, you will never be able to return. This is the end of your journey. Once you cross this river, you will be at peace, free from fear and pain.

But once you cross this river, you will never be able to see those you love again.

You imagine how everyone you know will feel when they learn about your passing. What will they say about you? Will they say you lived a good life? Will they say you always tried to do your best?

You think about the decisions you made that you regret. How did you learn from those experiences? How did you use them to do better in the future?

Now think about the moments when you were at your happiest and felt content. What were you doing? How could you have brought more happiness into your life?

The ferryman beckons to you again, but you shake your head. Now is not your time to travel with him.

He nods, knowing you will return to this place again.

You feel yourself travelling back to your body. Take a moment to appreciate the simple fact you are alive at this time, with a future of possibility ahead of you.

Notice your breath again, feeling gratitude for your life as you inhale and exhale.

And when you are ready, open your eyes.

Summary

Reflect on your own mortality on a regular basis. This will help you appreciate what you have all the more.

- Read biographies and autobiographies about death and dying.
- Plan your funeral and write your own eulogy.
- At the end of every day, take a moment to look back and reflect.
- Meditate on your mortality.

CHAPTER SIX

EMBRACE YOUR LACK OF CONTROL

"Sickness is a hindrance to the body, but not to your ability to choose, unless that is your choice. Lameness is a hindrance to the leg, but not to your ability to choose. Say this to yourself with regard to everything that happens, then you will see such obstacles as hindrances to something else, but not to yourself."
—Epictetus

How do you react when you find yourself stuck in traffic? Do you get impatient or angry? Do you yell at the cars in front of you, hoping they'll move?

Or what about when an activity you were looking forward to is cancelled because of the weather? Do you shake your fist at the sky, cursing the rain? Do you hurl abuse at the person who made the judgement call to cancel the event?

Does any of that change anything?

One of the most important aspects of living a Stoic life is recognising what you can and cannot change. Wasting energy on getting angry or upset with things that are outside of your control is futile when that energy could be better spent on the things you *can* control.

Whenever you face a difficult situation and your automatic response is to get angry or upset, ask yourself whether an emotional response will help you. Will it change the situation? Is the situation something you have any control over or is the only control you have your reaction?

When someone says or does something to you, it is your choice to decide that they are being insulting, offensive or audacious. As Epictetus noted, it isn't any particular event which upsets us, but our judgement about that event. Someone saying something you find hurtful has just uttered a few words. It is your choice to be hurt by them. When you get offended by someone, you have made yourself their accomplice. You have chosen to go along with their narrative and allowed yourself to be hurt.

It is incredibly liberating to realise that you have the power over whether you're upset or not. You have the freedom to ignore what someone is saying, go along with what they want you to do or politely respond. You do not have to buy in to what they're selling.

You have the power to move on. It is entirely up to you whether you use it or not.

The more intentional you can be with your reactions, the more Stoic you become. You should aim for an objective passivity in any trying situation before you decide what to do with it. The more you recognise which aspects of your life are outside of your control, the more you can let them go and focus on what you can change. Not only will this make you a happier person, it will give you a step up over others who are still caught up in this pointless struggle.

Practical Exercises

❖ *Start your day with a mantra.* Every morning, look at yourself in the mirror and recite this quote from Epictetus: "Some things are in our control and others not. Things in our control are opinion, pursuit, desire, aversion, and, in a word, whatever are our own actions. Things not in our control are body, property, reputation, command, and, in one word, whatever are not our own actions."

❖ *Don't ask yourself what would Jesus do; ask, what would my best self do?* We all have a vision of ourselves as we would like to be, that perfect person we could be if we weren't always tired or grumpy or overworked. Our best self eats properly, gets plenty of fresh air and exercise, doesn't procrastinate, is supportive and understanding of our loved ones and is a thoroughly good egg.

You do not have to wait for things to change to become that best self. You can be the best possible you right now. All you have to do is ask yourself, *what would my best self do?* in any given situation.

This is a useful practice in all situations, not just when you're facing a major issue. When you are honest about what your best self would do, you can consciously make the decision to *be* that best self – or recognise that you still have some work to do.

A few examples:

- Would my best self skip breakfast?
- Would my best self have hummus or a burger for lunch?
- Would my best self call my parents regularly?
- Would my best self actively reach out to friends beyond liking a few social media posts?
- Would my best self make the time to read a bedtime story to my children every night?
- Would my best self read a book or binge watch a Netflix series?
- Would my best self surf the internet during work?
- Would my best self hurl insults at the driver who cut me off on my way to work?
- Would my best self organise a babysitter so I can go out on a date with my partner?

- Would my best self drink wine every night?
- Would my best self go to the gym on a Saturday morning or stay in bed?

When you start asking yourself this question, it soon becomes clear what you need to do to be your best self. And it's okay if you can't be your best self all the time. We're only human and it takes persistent effort to be your best at every opportunity. But when you know what you should be doing, it becomes easier to move towards consciously making the best choice more often so you can start embodying your best self.

Summary

Strive to make good choices about the things that are under your control. Let go of any emotional attachment or response to the things you can't control.

- Start every day with a mantra.
- When faced with a choice, no matter how trivial or important, ask yourself, *what would my best self do?*

CHAPTER SEVEN

WORK WITHOUT LUST FOR RESULT

"Curb your desire—don't set your heart on so many things and you will get what you need."
—Epictetus

We've already discussed why it's important to differentiate between those things we can control and those we can't, and focusing our attention on the latter. However, while this is easy in theory, in practise it can be difficult to let go of our attachment to things we believe we can control, such as our career, our relationships, our environment, etc.

Yet our control over events around us is far less powerful than you suppose. Let's assume you've decided to join a five-a-side football club and you set yourself the target of scoring a goal at your first match. You might be an amazing footballer, but there are a number of factors that influence whether you'll succeed or fail, none of which is in your control.

The weather might be bad, which affects the quality of the pitch and how easy it is for you to play. Your shoelace might come undone so you trip at an inopportune moment. The opposing team might have trained harder than you or simply be the better team. You might fall badly and injure yourself so you have to leave the game.

None of these things is within your control, but can all mean you fail to achieve your goal. And having set yourself up to succeed, you're going to be disappointed when you don't.

This is why it's so important to *only* focus on what you can control – yourself.

So when you set goals, move away from thinking about results, which can be affected by external circumstances you cannot predict or affect. Instead, confine yourself solely to goals that are linked to your own efforts and ability. So, instead of having a target of scoring a goal, make it linked to training as much as possible, preparing yourself physically and mentally as much as possible, and promise yourself you'll do your very best during the match. You can do all of those things and still not score or win the match, but you've done everything possible to maximise your chances, so it's pointless wasting your energy on worrying about the result.

The effort is what's important.

You can apply this to every aspect of your life. So if, for example, you're job hunting, rather than making it a goal to get a specific job, which may or may not be the right job for you, make it your goal to research the company you're interviewing with, prepare answers to questions you're likely to be asked, etc. to give yourself the best possible chance of getting the job. You may well not get the job despite all of that effort, but if you've prepared as well as you can, the Stoic belief is that it wasn't meant to be.

Or let's assume you're single and want to be in a relationship. Instead of focusing on finding someone and risking your desperation scaring people away, focus on making yourself someone people would like to be in a relationship with. Dress well, get a good haircut, go out to places where you might meet someone you're interested in being with – but if you don't, you'll still have a good time.

When I wrote this book, I didn't set a goal around how many copies I wanted to sell. I can't control that figure. But I made my goal to research this book, put together material people would find truly valuable and write something people enjoy reading that gives the reader useful exercises to help them take a Stoic approach to life. Then I had a goal of organising my marketing and advertising campaigns so I could tell as many people as possible about my book. So while I might not know how many books I'll sell, I'll give myself a good chance of healthy sales.

Whether you've set yourself goals or not in the past, now is a good time to get into the habit. When you set goals in your personal life, you support yourself in creating your dream life. If you connect your goals to your effort and mindset (the things you can control), you have a much greater chance of getting to where you need to be – but you don't attach any emotion to that destination, recognising that it's the journey that matters, and the journey is where you learn and grow.

Practical Exercises

> *Examine your Wheel of Life.* Draw a circle and divide it up into segments. Now label each segment according to a different area of your life, e.g. family, friends, relationship, career, social life, spiritual life, etc. In each segment, write out where you would like to be and where you currently are.
>   • What do you notice? Which areas of your life need attention? Which parts are you happy with and don't want to change?
>   • When you take a moment to examine your life dispassionately, it helps you see where you should be focusing your attention and what needs work.
> *Set yourself goals and hold yourself accountable to them.* When you've created your Wheel of Life, it's very easy to see what kind of goals you should be setting. However, the key thing here is to keep your focus on your own effort rather than results. So,

for example, let's say you want to set up a business and make a certain amount of money from it. You can't guarantee how much money you'll make, but you can certainly break down the steps you need to work through to set up a business and then plan out what you need to do to make money from that business. So, if you're selling a product, you can have an advertising plan, or if you're selling a service, you can have a goal of reaching out to a certain number of potential clients with an offer.

Once you've set your goals, you need to keep yourself on track. You do this by checking in with yourself on a daily, weekly and quarterly basis. At the beginning of every day, briefly summarise the past 24 hours and write out what you're going to do that day to move closer to your goals. You might not work towards every single goal every day, but you should be making effort towards at least one of them. Once a week, go over all your goals and note your progress. This will help you see where you're falling behind so you can adjust what you're doing moving forward. Then, every quarter, review how far you've come and adjust your goals and plans where necessary to continue to move forward.

At the end of a twelve-month cycle, redo your goals. It may well be that you haven't achieved everything you set out to do, and this is okay. You will have learned a lot about yourself and your priorities in the process, and you will have discovered what works for you and what doesn't.

And the best part? When you set a goal attached to effort rather than outcome, progress is inevitable. While you might not end up where you intend to be, you'll find your life changes in so many positive ways, it really doesn't matter whether you get to where you wanted to go.

Summary

While goal setting is important, you need to make sure your goals are focused on effort rather than targets. You cannot fully control whether you meet your goals, but you have total control over your own attitude and whether you work hard or not.

- Examine your Wheel of Life.
- Set goals and hold yourself accountable to them.

CHAPTER EIGHT

THE POWER OF JOURNALING

"There is indeed a limit fixed for us, just where the remorseless law of Fate has fixed it; but none of us knows how near he is to this limit. Therefore, let us so order our minds as if we had come to the very end... Let us balance life's account every day... One who daily puts the finishing touches to his life is never in want of time."
—Seneca

M any of the Stoics whose writing inspire us today were avid diarists. Epictetus, Marcus Aurelius and Seneca all journaled regularly, Epictetus telling his students that they should "write down day by day" their thoughts on philosophy to "exercise themselves." Seneca would write in his journal every night after his wife had gone to bed. He said he would "examine my entire day and go back over what I've done and said, hiding nothing from myself, passing nothing by." He also remarked that after he'd carried out this serious self-reflection, he slept particularly soundly.

And it is most noteworthy to recognise that Aurelius entitled his journals as "to himself." A prolific journaler, Aurelius considered this process absolutely essential in his life.

In order for journaling to fulfil the purpose you need it to, it needs to go beyond simply noting down the events of the day. After all, this is a philosophical practice, so it is not enough to only list what happened.

As a Stoic, when you journal, you should consider what happened that day and what lessons you learned. You should also be thinking about the next day and how you can prepare for it. Consider your studies of Stoicism – are you reading any books written by the Classic scholars? Researching the philosophy further? Record your observations and personal experiences of applying their lessons.

Living a Stoic life is an ongoing process. It is not enough to read a few books and consider yourself a master. You need to put them into practice and then consistently reflect on how you're doing and make a conscious effort to improve your attitude and outlook to become the best possible person you can be.

Journaling allows you to reflect on how successful you are in applying everything you've learned and how you can continue to apply those lessons.

As if that wasn't enough, there are many other reasons why journaling is a positive habit for you to develop.

- *Journaling reduces stress.* Modern living is incredibly stressful and anything you can do to reduce that stress must be a good thing. There have been many studies that have shown that journaling is a great way to help you manage stress. Indeed, if you journal just a couple of times a week for 15-20 minutes, you can bring down your blood pressure and improve your liver function. (If you don't believe me, just check out https://www.mic.com/articles/110662/science-shows-something-surprising-about-people-who-still-journal for all the references and other proven health benefits!) Choose a time of day that is best for you. This could be first thing in the morning or last thing at night. Journaling at the same time every day will help you establish it as a habit and help you focus your mind where it needs to be.
- *Journaling improves your memory.* On the one hand, it seems like a no-brainer that journaling will help you remember things. After all, you've got a written record of your experiences, so even if you can't recall exactly what happened, you can look back over your notes to remind yourself. But it would seem that the act of recording your life on a daily basis helps you get better at remembering things in

general, improving your memory and potentially even helping your brain's cognitive processes.

- *Journaling puts you in a better mood.* One of the many benefits of journaling is that it can help you retain a more positive outlook on life and improve your emotional wellbeing.

- *Journaling makes you more self-aware.* It should be unsurprising that when you regularly reflect on life's events and how they make you feel, you develop a stronger understanding of who you are. The more you journal, the more you connect with your inner needs and drives while retaining perspective. It also helps you cope during difficult times and transitions, supporting you in identifying pivotal times and going with the flow. Even if you're not a creative type, journaling helps develop your creativity, bringing out more of your brainpower.

Realistically, there's no reason not to journal and countless reasons to get started.

Practical exercises

Just get started. Journaling will come more easily to some people than others. The very thought of writing anything might fill you with dread. But I'd refer you to the first chapter where you were told to push yourself out of your comfort zone – if journaling makes you feel uncomfortable, good!

Buy yourself a nice notebook, something that you find attractive and makes you want to fill it with your thoughts. Journaling by hand is a much more immersive experience. When you physically write your words, it stimulates your brain in a way that typing on a computer just cannot.

Then write something. Anything. Even if you only write one sentence a day, promise yourself you'll do that much/little. That sentence could sum up the past 24 hours; it could detail what you had for dinner. It doesn't matter what you say as long as you say *something*. Once you've established the habit, you can then develop it further to be more reflective.

And most importantly, switch off your inner critic. No one is going to be reading your journal other than you. It doesn't matter whether your spelling is correct or your grammar is perfect. All that matters is that you've journaled.

Write every day. There is no excuse. You can find time to write a single sentence every day. If that is all you write, that is more than enough to get started and you'll find that sentence organically grows into more.

If you need a prompt to get you started, here are a few questions for you:

- What was the most significant event of the past 24 hours? How did it make you feel?

- What are you currently reading? Are there any important lessons you've learned from the book?
- What are you grateful for? Can you list at least three things?
- If you've followed the earlier exercises in the book, you should have some goals you're working towards. What did/can you do to move closer to those goals?

Summarise your week. Once a week, do a more in-depth journaling session to review the previous week and examine your progress towards a more Stoic life. If you have goals, chart what you've done towards them and see what needs prioritising for the coming week.

Make a note of the biggest lesson you've learned that week and how you're applying your Stoic studies to your life, as well as how things are changing for the better as a result of a Stoic attitude.

Summary

Journaling has many valuable health benefits, as well as being an important part of a Stoic lifestyle. You should keep a journal to help you deepen your understandings and Stoic practices.

- Just get started. It is more important to document your thoughts than to worry about crafting beautiful prose.

- Write every day.
- Take things a step further and summarise your week in detail.

CHAPTER NINE

PREPARE FOR THE WORST

*"Nothing happens to the wise man against his
expectation… nor do all things turn out for him
as he wished but as he reckoned—and above all he
reckoned that something could block his plans."*
—Seneca

There is a Stoic practice known as 'premeditatio malorum.' Literally translated this means 'the pre-meditation of evils' and involves visualising everything that could go wrong or losing everything that is important to you. After all, as they say, life is what happens when you're busy making plans. You can have everything worked out to the finest detail only to have the rug pulled out from under you by a nasty accident, job loss or relationship breakup. It doesn't matter how hard we work; we don't always get what we deserve, no matter how much we've earned it.

Premeditatio malorum, or what we might call now 'negative visualisation,' means you can mentally prepare for the worst because, at some point in our lives, bad things will happen. For a Stoic, this is not a negative thing because you've anticipated this and have the resilience and fortitude to withstand all the slings and arrows life can throw at you. Not only do you develop mental strength, you also develop a renewed appreciation of all the blessings in your life, which you may not currently recognise.

It is important to walk a fine line between anticipating trouble and becoming consumed by stress and worry. When you practice negative visualisation, this shouldn't be done with a mindset of 'this is what's definitely going to happen.' It's more a case that you simply can't know what's going to happen, so you're open to all possibilities.

Look at it another way. Is a glass filled to half its capacity half empty or half full? To a Stoic, neither would be the case. The Stoic interpretation is that there is water to drink, so be grateful for it. And the fact that the water is contained within a glass? Bonus!

So, when you visualise losing your family, you're not doing this because you genuinely believe they're going to die. But the knowledge that they might not always be there will help you be grateful for their presence in your life and have more patience on those days when things aren't going well and there's friction among all of you. Done properly, negative visualisation will help you feel true gratitude for the blessings your life enjoys, whether that be financial success, a happy marriage, or simply the feel of the sun on your face as you walk outside.

When we anticipate tough times and use that visualisation as a spur to squeeze every benefit from every second life gives us, we remove most, if not all, of the power negative events have to devastate us. Change is inevitable and not always for the good; but when we lose something or someone important to us, that loss isn't as overwhelming when we are armed with the knowledge that we really did embrace every possible ounce of happiness while we could.

Practical exercises

❖ *Journal it out.* Writing out a list of everything that could go wrong and the potential consequences is a good way of getting things clear in your head. It can also help you come up with contingency plans and even make preparations to mitigate the impact of the worst things.

Pick an event you have coming up and list everything that could possibly go wrong or even stop it from happening altogether. For example, if you have a holiday booked, your list might include:
- Losing your passport.
- Your flights being cancelled.
- Your luggage being lost.
- Extreme weather, e.g. hurricanes, storms.

- Natural disasters.
- Being robbed.
- Getting food poisoning.
- Getting severely sunburnt.
- Having an accident during an exciting activity.

I'm sure you can think of many more things that could go wrong, so make your list as long as you possibly can. Don't worry about including items that are highly unlikely – they're still possible and the point of this exercise is to prepare yourself for *every* eventuality.

Once you've completed your list, go back and document how it would make you feel if that happened. Really immerse yourself in that feeling, as if you're experiencing it right now, so should that event actually occur, you already know how you'd deal with it.

Finally, for each item, note what you could do to either minimise the likelihood of it occurring or, if it's outside of your control (as most things are), what you can do to minimise its disruption to your trip. By doing this, you've prepared yourself for the worst – but also allowed for the possibility of the best, because if nothing on your list happens, you'll feel grateful for a stress-free break. You'll enjoy your holiday all the more because you'll have a full understanding of how bad it could have been, so you'll be motivated to have as much fun as you can throughout your entire trip.

❖ *Meditate on the worst.* While brainstorming every negative possibility is a valuable exercise, you'll also find it helpful to practise actual visualisation to experience the event as if it were happening right now. Done properly, this is a very emotional experience, so make sure you choose a time and place for this exercise where you won't be disturbed and can immerse yourself in the moment without feeling like you have to self-censor for the sake of those around you.

Choose one of the worst things you could experience. It might be losing a loved one; it could be experiencing a life-changing accident. Perhaps you want to think about becoming homeless following a redundancy. Pick something which is your absolute worst nightmare, the one thing you really *don't* want to see come true.

Sit yourself comfortably, making sure your back is supported, so you can meditate without being distracted by your body needing to fidget. Close your eyes and imagine someone telling you the news you didn't want to hear. Picture their face, the sadness in their eyes as they tell you what happened and how sorry they are for you. Allow yourself to be flooded with emotion as you feel denial it could be possible, anger that it's happened, sadness that things will never be the same again. If you need to cry, cry.

Don't think about what to do next. This is not the time to come up with contingency plans. Instead, immerse yourself completely in the feelings of the moment. Know that there was absolutely nothing you could have done to change this outcome, so all you can do is accept that this is how it is and adjust your reality accordingly.

This too will pass. No matter how badly you feel in the moment, this moment is not forever.

Summary

Regularly visualise worst-case scenarios to help plan and prepare, as well as develop the mental resilience to cope with it.

- Journal what could happen and how you'll deal with it.
- Meditate on your worst nightmare and fully immerse yourself in the emotions arising from that.

CHAPTER TEN

AMOR FATI

"All that is in accord with you is in accord with me,
O World! Nothing which occurs at the right time
for you comes too soon or too late for me. All that
your seasons produce, O Nature, is fruit for me.
It is from you that all things come: all things are
within you, and all things move toward you."
—Marcus Aurelius

The term '*amor fati*' is most commonly associated with Friedrich Nietzsche, who used it to denote a love of fate we should all aspire to. In his book, *Ecce Homo: How One Becomes What Is,* he wrote, "My formula for greatness in a human being is *amor fati*: that one wants nothing to be different, not forward, not backward, not in all eternity. Not merely bear what is necessary, still less conceal it—all idealism is mendacity in the face of what is necessary—but love it."

However, while he may have popularised this attitude, it was one very popular with the Stoics a couple of thousand years ago. Marcus Aurelius wrote, "A blazing fire makes flame and brightness out of everything that is thrown into it," meaning that it doesn't matter what happens – if you have the right state of being, whatever comes your way will be transformed and assimilated into your life experiences.

Essentially, *amor fati* is the attitude that regardless of what comes your way, every experience is to be welcomed and accepted, regardless of whether it appears to be positive or negative. When it comes to challenges, *amor fati* goes beyond simple acceptance. You should love whatever difficulties you face because they are what forge you into a better person. So just like fuel for a fire, those tough times are fuel for your personal growth.

We discussed earlier how little is within your control and that principle is the foundation to *amor fati*. Because the only things you have true control over are your thoughts and deeds, the faster you can fully assimilate that into your philosophy of life, the faster you can move past anger, frustration or misery when the universe throws you a curveball. It is deeply empowering to know that you have the ability to make the most of the events in your life, no matter what. The very notion of fate, which is tied up in the concept of *amor fati*, means that we have no control over our destinies. All we can do is love the life we're given.

Most of us are pessimists. We feel that things are going to go wrong sooner or later while the good things in life have to be worked for and can be taken away at any moment. Yet we fight against that, trying to control the uncontrollable. This is why so many of us are unhappy with our lot. We're trying to swim upstream against the flow.

When you accept that difficulties are going to come, you have a choice. Resent that and continue to be unhappy, or love the challenges they give you and the chances they provide for you to grow, adapt and evolve. While everything may be fated on some level, *amor fati* means that everything happens for a reason, but it's entirely up to you to decide on what that reason will be. Is it to make you miserable or is it to give you opportunities you could never have imagined?

Practical Exercises

✓ *Journal your thought process.* Again, your journal is an important part of developing the right mindset.

Look back on everything you've documented so far. Highlight those times when you were able to utilise a Stoic acceptance of what was going on around you and the difference this made to your reactions. Think about how you would have reacted to that situation before you started following a Stoic path.

Choose a Stoic quote that sums up *amor fati* for you and write your thoughts on what it means and how you can incorporate it into your practises. Do you think this will be easy or difficult for you? What challenges can you anticipate and how can you overcome them?

✓ *Keep your mind on the right track.* Training your mind is one of the hardest things you can do. You can promise yourself as much as you like that you're going to accept the present as it comes, but you'll soon find yourself slipping into hoping the future will be the way you want, or wishing the past had been different.

So every morning, when you wake up, say to yourself, "I accept today as it is, not as I would like it to be." Whenever you notice yourself sliding into thinking about the future or the past, repeat this mantra to bring your attention back to the present.

One way you can support this process is by wearing an elastic band around your wrist. Every time your thoughts stray away from the present, ping the band against your wrist so that you experience a mild discomfort. This will help you keep your attention where it needs to be.

✓ *Stop complaining.* Do you know someone who does nothing but complain about how much they hate their job but when you suggest they find another one, they come up with a million reasons why they can't? How frustrating is it? The solution to their problem is right there, but they'd rather complain than take actual steps to improve their situation.

It's a natural human reaction to complain, and airing our grievances is healthy. However, when we get stuck in a cycle of complaining, we waste energy we could be putting towards improving our lot. What's more, complaining doesn't actually make you feel better. It just reminds you about how bad things are. And the reality is, there's not a lot that happens we can't do something about.

Accepting what comes without complaint doesn't mean you passively lie back and let people walk all over you. Instead, it means you dispassionately observe whatever situation you find yourself in and look for the opportunity in the obstacle.

So if you break your arm, you don't complain it's hurting but do nothing to fix it. You get yourself to A&E and get it set. You accept you won't be typing much for the next few weeks. You think about installing dictation software to help you with your workload. (You may even find you like it so much that you continue using it after your arm is healed!) You take it as a sign to slow down and maybe read a few books on Stoicism while you heal.

See if you can go a whole week without complaining once. And if that's too much, start with a day and build on that. Journal the process and note how many times you complain so you can work on reducing that number.

✓ *Talk to your future self.* When the printer jams or someone cuts in front of you on the motorway, it can make your blood boil. But if you took a moment to think about how that's going to affect your future, the reality is it really isn't that big of a deal. You can unclog the printer and get on with your work. The chances are high you'll overtake the person who raced past you as you get further down the motorway – and even if you don't, you'll still arrive at your destination when you need.

Very little will negatively impact your future if you take a moment to breathe and consider just how important your frustrations are. Even major events lose their impact over you given enough time. That nasty breakup probably won't be haunting you five years from now when you're happily married to the love of your life. That embarrassing foot-in-mouth moment when you said something stupid in an interview for your dream job won't be important when you're running your own company a few years down the line.

It doesn't matter what it is. When something negative happens, ask yourself, "How will I be feeling about this event in ten years' time?" The reality is that in almost every single instance, the answer will be "I won't feel this bad." That doesn't mean you won't always mourn the loss of a parent, for example, but you won't feel their loss so intensely.

You shouldn't punish your future self because of things you are experiencing now. Eventually, you'll be able to put it into perspective and accept it as another one of life's myriad lessons. Whatever happens, it could always be worse.

Another way of looking at it is to think about what advice you'd give to a friend who was going through what you're going through. Realistically, you're likely to be telling them not to worry, that everything's going to be all right, it'll all work out in the end.

✓ *Life is a game, so play it with all your heart.* Whether you're a Candy Crush fan or a hard-core gamer, the one thing you want from a game is that it challenges you. There's a buzz that comes from winning that difficult level or beating that tough opponent you simply don't get when the game is easy.

It's the same with life. Sure, you may not understand all the rules, and there are parts that may not make sense to you, but that's the playing field you're on. The Stoic approach is to accept that the rules are random, but play the game as hard as you can. Win or lose, it's all about the experience. While setbacks can be frustrating, if you see it as part of the game you need to beat in order to level up, you're a long way towards being Stoic.

✓ *Be grateful for whatever happens.* It's easy to be grateful for the blessings we have. It can be much more difficult to be grateful for the hardships, but it's important you feel just as thankful for the bad things in life as the good.

One piece of advice I was given by my dad really resonated with me and is very relevant here. He said that when you first hold your child in your arms, you want to protect them from anything bad that can happen, but that's doing them a disservice. The times when you've grown the most have been when you've been challenged. Why would you deprive your child of that lesson?

When we're in the middle of a difficult time, we feel that our emotional response is the 'correct' one. We feel it's the only logical, natural reaction, yet if you ask your future self what good things came out of that moment, the bigger picture shows us that there was a lot of positive to love in that moment, even if it didn't feel like it.

Maybe your car won't start so you're going to be late for work. Frustrating, right? But what if there had been a major accident on your route and if you'd left on time, you'd have been involved in it and potentially suffered serious injuries? Your car not starting suddenly becomes a blessing.

While we can't know what would have happened if we had done something different, we can trust that the path we're on is the right one for us and the problems we have are meant to teach us something valuable. So be grateful for them, because if you really want to be your authentic, powerful self, you'll love whatever comes your way because every single event is an opportunity to make your life even better.

Summary

Love all aspects of your life, the ups and the downs, because everything is a lesson and helps you grow into a better person.

- Use your journal to help you appreciate your life.
- Keep your mind focused on the present moment.
- Stop complaining.
- Put things in perspective by talking to your future self.
- Treat life as a game and play it to the best of your ability.
- Be grateful for everything you have, good and bad.

CHAPTER ELEVEN

TIME IS ON YOUR SIDE

"Begin at once to live, and count each
separate day as a separate life."
—*Seneca*

W ith all the exercises you've been give so far in this book, you may be feeling a little overwhelmed by this point, so now's a good time to remind you to breathe. At its essence, Stoicism is a very simple, practical philosophy.

Seneca's essay '*De Brevitate Vitae*' (On the Shortness of Life) discusses the fact that people waste a lot of their time engaging in meaningless pursuits. His argument is that we are all given enough time to do what is truly important, so it is up to us to make appropriate use of however long we have on this earth. He felt that the best use of our time was to live in the present moment with an intentional, purposeful attitude.

Most people waste their time, according to Seneca. We cannot afford to do anything other than live in the now because tomorrow could be too late. We never know when our time here is up, but for the Stoic, this is not a bad thing because they are always ready to take their last breath, as they have the reassurance of knowing they've always valued the gifts of life. In comparison, most people stress about how short life is because they're obsessing about the bad things that have happened in the past, worried about what the future will bring, failing to notice what's going on in front of them right now.

Seneca states that we waste time because we don't value it in the way we do our money or things. After all, it's difficult to pin down time. It slips through our fingers when we try to hold onto it and it doesn't have any tangible properties, so we're happy to give it away to others who want it from us because we don't see its worth.

To a Stoic, time is the most valuable thing you have, if not the *only* thing, so you need to live in the present with purpose and in harmony with Nature. Not only does this ground you in the current moment, it also gives you power over both the past and future, empowering you to be truly free and happy.

We've already touched on mindfulness and will be delving into it in greater depth in the next chapter, but it's worth mentioning again because this is key to making the most of your time. When you set your intention to be fully aware of everything you do and pay attention to your thoughts and actions, you open yourself up to unexpected possibilities. Not only that, you find yourself becoming more creative, more thoughtful and engaged in the world around you. When you are mindful of wanting to benefit from every waking moment, sleep becomes the last thing you want to do because there's so much more to experience.

If you've been sleepwalking through life, now's the time to wake up.

Although Stoicism encourages a detachment from material things and tough times, this does not mean you become indifferent to them. Instead, you reprioritise your expectations so you're focusing on being your best self rather than feeding your ego. When you are your best, success naturally follows without your putting effort or attachment into the result, which is one of the most empowering feelings you can experience.

Pursuing money, status and material possessions is not the Stoic way. The only thing worth chasing is virtue. Wisdom, justice, self-awareness, bravery – *these* are the goals you should be aiming for. After all, you could have all the money in the world and still be miserable. You could be highly educated with multiple doctorates yet be a deeply unpleasant person supporting an unjust system that favours the rich over the poor.

As Marcus Aurelius put it, "A branch cut from its neighbouring branch is necessarily cut away from the whole tree. In the same way a human being severed from just one other human has dropped from the whole community. Now the branch is cut off by someone else, but a man separates himself from his neighbour by his own hatred or rejection, not realising that he has thereby severed himself from the wider society of fellow citizens. Only there is this gift we have from Zeus who brought together the human community: we can grow back again to our neighbour and resume our place in the complement of the whole."

While it is only natural to feel a greater loyalty to our friends and family than the populace at large, Stoicism teaches that we're all part of a universal citizenship, so while we might think local, everything we do is a global act because when we focus on living a virtuous life and treating those around us with respect, this creates a ripple effect, building a society that is harmonious instead of selfish.

We looked at how you can turn obstacles into opportunities, but this isn't just something to do by yourself. Collectively, society as a whole can do this together. It's very easy to believe there's nothing you can do as an individual to improve the world at large, but little things add up. You can choose where you spend your money, the kind of food you buy, the type of car you drive (or if you even drive at all), what clothes you wear, etc. All of these choices are an expression of your beliefs and values, so now is the time to be more intentional in your consumerism.

As a Stoic, it is your responsibility to question whether you truly need to buy something and, if you do, where you should source it. Purchasing something you don't really need doesn't just undermine your personal path to virtue; it also undermines society's. If you don't choose ethical suppliers, you're supporting the use of sweatshops and slavery, the destruction of the rainforest and unethical behaviour by big corporations.

It would be a mistake to assume that Stoicism is anti-capitalism. Stoicism transcends politics and eschews a dogged adherence to any specific political ideology. Instead, it takes a more pragmatic approach. Reason does not have a political leaning, so it is for a Stoic to look at the facts of any given situation and follow where reason takes him. It is up to you to define what you view as reasonable and just and champion that. It is also your responsibility to combat inequality and immorality as best you can in whatever way makes most sense to you. This is still your personal path and it is up to you to define it in the manner that makes most sense according to your unique experience.

Or, to quote Marcus Aurelius again, "Do only what the reasons inherent in kingly and judicial powers prescribe for the benefit of mankind… change your ground, if in fact there is someone to correct and guide you away from some notion. But this transference must always spring from a conviction of justice or the common good:

and your preferred course must be likewise, not simply for apparent pleasure or popularity."

It takes courage to stand up when we see someone being racist or sexist. It takes wisdom to navigate the nuances of societal expectations and norms to see where true inequality exists, let alone come up with a way of combating it. But as a Stoic, it is your duty to do so, so that we can transform society to a more just and equitable one. It is, quite simply, the right thing to do.

Practical Exercises

> *Become an intentional consumer.* It is impossible to live in our modern time and not cause harm in one form or another. Unless you walk everywhere, your choice of transport contributes to pollution. Unless you grow your own food, everything you eat has a carbon footprint. You can drive yourself insane worrying about the damage your mere existence is doing with every breath.
>
> What's more, there are also budgetary concerns. It's great to want to only eat organic, but if you can't afford it, you shouldn't starve yourself.
>
> Stoicism is a journey that comes with the understanding that you can only do your best. If someone is a more ethical consumer than you, so what? Start small. Plan out your meals for the week so you can plan your purchases. Consider eating

food that is in season, so you only buy items you can source locally. If you can afford to, shop at the local market or small, family-owned businesses rather than large supermarkets.

Or look at your toiletries. Are you buying from companies with an ethical attitude towards their products? Is your shampoo biodegradable? Does your soap contain palm oil? Educate yourself about the products you buy and look into alternatives if you discover you can do better.

➤ *Give time, not money, to charities.* It's easy to think that you've done your bit to be virtuous by donating to a worthy cause. But it's our time that is the most valuable thing we have. Spend it wisely by giving it to a local charity whose aims you support. Maybe you could clean up a local beauty spot or visit an old people's home. Look for something you will find rewarding and enjoyable, as well as genuinely improving your little corner of the world.

Many large charities do not spend their funds in the most ethical manner, and instead operate in a way that is more akin to big business than in keeping with their philanthropic aims. Small, local charities are far more likely to be in need of your help and will be all the more appreciative of it. What's more, you'll be able to see the results of your efforts and know you're genuinely making a difference. While you shouldn't be doing this to fuel your ego, having direct experience of helping others brings with it the feel-good factor and incentivises you to do even more.

Summary

Time is our most valuable possession. Spend it wisely and focus your efforts on living a virtuous life that contributes to a just, equitable society.

- Shop ethically and intentionally.
- Donate your time to charity instead of money.

CHAPTER TWELVE

TAKE A STOIC APPROACH TO MINDFULNESS

*"Every hour focus your mind attentively…on the
performance of the task in hand, with dignity, human
sympathy, benevolence and freedom, and leave aside
all other thoughts. You will achieve this, if you
perform each action as if it were your last…"*
—Marcus Aurelius

We've touched upon mindfulness in previous chapters. Now it's time to really dig deep into the topic.

Why is mindfulness so important? To quote Marcus Aurelius again, "Each man only lives in this present instant…all the rest either has been lived or remains in uncertainty." This ties in very much with the Stoic approach to life. If all we possess is this present moment, it makes sense to focus all our attention on it. While the ancient Stoics might not have dubbed their attitude mindfulness, in a modern context, it's a similar principle.

Epictetus talks about '*prosoche*' in his texts. Roughly translated as 'attention,' he argues that *prosoche* is essential for anyone wishing to live an ethical life and that it doesn't matter what you're doing; even singing along to the radio or reading a book can – and should – be done with *prosoche*. He felt that once you've let your mind go off in whatever direction it wants, you've lost power to keep it directed at what's right. Your mind needs to be geared towards moderation and self-awareness at all times.

On the surface, this seems like hard work. Needing to constantly keep your mind focused on the now without straying towards the past or future requires continual effort, and the very thought can be daunting, let alone starting the process.

But Stoicism is a journey. It's okay to stumble along the way. You don't have to be a master. You just have to do your best and know that the more you do, the better you become.

Remember, focus on what you can control and don't worry about what you can't. The more you do this, the easier it becomes to be mindful in your actions. As you make your way through your day, ask yourself, "How am I handling this situation? Am I focused on what I can control or am I letting what I cannot control overwhelm my thoughts?"

Let's look at a few examples. Let's say you are put in charge of putting together an important presentation at work. You know that if you do well, your manager will be happy with you and if you don't, she'll disapprove. You could even be demoted or promoted as a consequence of how the presentation goes.

A natural instinct would be to work with your manager's approval in mind. Your goal would be to make them happy, but as a Stoic, you should appreciate that their happiness is outside of your control. You cannot choose whether someone feels happy or not. All you can do is do your job to the best of your abilities without attaching any importance to winning the approval of your manager. Of course, if you do the presentation well, the chances are high that your manager will be happy with you, but that is a side effect. What is in your control is the amount of effort you put into the presentation, developing a good relationship with your manager so you know what they are looking for when reviewing your work, and focusing on working to the best of your abilities – or even seeking training to improve your skills. *These* are the things you can control. Your manager's feelings are not among them.

Epictetus gave another example of this principle in play when he discussed a singer suffering from stage fright. He wrote:

"When I see man in anxiety, I say to myself, 'What can it be that this fellow wants? For if he did not want something that was outside of his control, how could he still remain in anxiety? That is why when singing on his own he shows no anxiety, but does so what he enters the theatre, even though he has a beautiful voice. For he does not wish merely to sing well, but also to win applause, and that is no longer under his control… Why is this? Why, he simply does not know what a crowd is, or the applause of a crowd…hence he trembles and turn pale.'"

Epictetus argues that stage fright is all down to a fear of the audience not applauding the performance. So a vocalist with the wrong mindset will feel amazing if the crowd claps and cheers, but if they don't get the reaction they want, they'll feel depressed and likely suffer even greater stage fright next time.

In contrast, a Stoic singer doesn't place any importance on the audience's enjoyment of his performance. He just practises and prepares and sings to the best of his abilities, regardless of whether the audience likes his singing or not.

It doesn't matter what it is you're doing. If you worry about winning the approval of others, your focus is in the wrong place. And the beauty of paying attention to the things that are in your control, e.g. how hard you work, how easily you go with the flow, etc. is that all this effort is likely to mean you do a good job and make it far more likely you gain the support of others. Conversely, when you worry about what others think, you risk undermining your efforts because you're so worried about getting it 'right,' according to other's standards, that you can't do your best because you're too stressed.

When you are trying to change the way you think and reprogram your mind, it is important to maintain self-awareness so you don't fall into any of the potential pitfalls in your way. One possible issue with focusing on yourself is that you risk becoming selfish and not caring about what others think or feel. After all, their feelings are under their control and not your responsibility, right?

Yet if this is how you interpret this mindset, you've misunderstood what the Stoics were hoping to achieve. Remember, Stoicism isn't just about being your best self and living a virtuous life; this virtue is intended to build a better society, a community of people who are working together for the common good to create an environment which is positive for everyone involved.

It is your responsibility as a Stoic to remember that it is up to you how virtuous you are, that you have the choice to do the right thing that will benefit all concerned. When you do your best, this automatically helps everyone. You might not be aiming to make your manager happy, but if you've done your best and hit all your targets, by default your manager will be satisfied.

Under Stoicism, your relationships can only flourish when you actively choose to place your priorities where you can control what you do *and* combine it with an active aim to be a good person. In Epictetus' words, "For where one can say 'I' and 'mine,' to there will the human being incline. If 'I' and 'mine' are placed in the flesh, there will the human being's ruling power be; if they are in the moral purpose, there must it be; if they are in externals, there must it be. If, therefore, I am where my moral purpose is, then, and then only, will I be the friend and son and father that I should be. For then this will by interest – to keep my good faith, my self-respect, my forbearance, my co-cooperation, and to maintain my relationships with other human beings."

In other words, whatever you are giving attention to is what is going to manifest the most in your life. If you're stressing about external factors, they'll continue to rule you and you'll continue to be miserable and worried. If you're only concerned about your personal happiness, you'll miss the opportunity to grow into the valuable member of society you have the potential to be. But if you constantly strive to do your best by considering only those things you have control over, everyone benefits, not just you.

The ancient Stoics always looked to nature to inspire them and they believed that humans were designed by nature to live in harmony with each other. As the saying goes, it takes a village to raise a child, and the Stoics felt that if we are to live according to our nature, we should be caring and compassionate towards one another as a matter of course. Further, we should be doing the right thing because it is the right thing to do, not because we want to be applauded for it or have everyone see that we're 'good.' So, if you're volunteering with a local charity, the only reason you would have to tell others about it would be if you genuinely believed they may be able to help out at all. Otherwise, simply get on with the work and move from one good act to the next and the next.

Or, as Marcus Aurelius puts it, "Like the vine that produces its grapes, seeking nothing more once it has given forth its fruit…so the good man having done one deed well, does not shout it about, but turns to the next good deed, just like the vine turns to bear forth its fruit in due season."

So, while we can see modern mindfulness in the Stoic's approach, they take this further than simply living fully in the moment. You should be staying present *and* paying attention to what you can control and doing that to the best of your ability with a driving motivation of being kind towards your fellow man. Indeed, it was the Stoics who original coined the notion of a 'community of humankind.'

Practical Exercises

❖ *Check your focus.* Rather than waiting for an event to happen and take a reactive approach to maintaining your focus on what you can control, weave this attitude into your day until it becomes second nature. At regular intervals during the day, ask yourself, "Where is my focus?" You might find it useful to set an alarm to go off every hour to remind yourself to keep your attention in the right place. Remember, if something is outside of your control, it is not your business to give it any energy, freeing you up to give your all to the things you do have agency over.

❖ *Love everyone.* When someone undermines you at work or cuts in front of you when you're queuing, it's very difficult to remember that we should be acting with compassion towards everyone. This loving kindness meditation will help you practice love towards everyone, regardless of how they treat you. The more you recognise that everyone is worthy of love, the easier it becomes to act with kindness in accordance with your best self.

Make yourself comfortable with your back supported and close your eyes. Turn your attention to your breath and observe as you inhale and exhale... inhale and exhale...

And as you breathe, feel yourself filling with peace and perfect love. With every exhalation, breathe out your stress, fear and worry, and with every inhalation draw in more peace and love until you feel a deep, fulfilling calmness. Know that the universe loves you. You are worthy of love. You deserve peace and love at all times.

As you feel this beautiful sensation of calm and peace, think of someone you love, your partner, your children, your parents, a close friend. Whoever you think about, send that beautiful peace in their direction. See them being filled with love and harmony until they are as calm and happy as you are in this moment.

Do this again for all your close loved ones.

Now move on to people you are not so close to. Perhaps your colleagues, your neighbours, the person who regularly serves you at your favourite restaurant. Send this love and peace towards them, filling them up with calm, peace and contentment.

Finally, think about those who have done you wrong, those you do not like, those who have made your life difficult. They, too, deserve love, so send them the same waves of love and peace, accepting them for who they are and knowing that they are worthy of love because they have taught you valuable lessons and helped you become the person you are today.

When you have finished sending love to everyone who needs it, sit a little longer, feeling this beautiful, peaceful energy.

When you are ready, open your eyes, knowing that this love and peace is always with you.

Summary

Being Stoic in your mindfulness means that not only do you live in the present moment, you combine this with solely focusing on what is under your control and acting with love, kindness and compassion at all times.

- Regularly check your focus throughout the day so you only care about what you can control.
- Do the loving kindness meditation whenever you feel in need of extra love or need to remind yourself that we are all worthy of love.

CHAPTER THIRTEEN

EVERYTHING IN MODERATION

"In your actions, don't procrastinate. In your conversations, don't confuse. In your thoughts, don't wander. In your soul, don't be passive or aggressive. In your life, don't be all about business."
—Marcus Aurelius

The ancient Greeks and Romans were notorious for their huge parties. So many movies depict decadent orgies, massive indulgences in the pleasures of the flesh, symbolic of a society that knew how to celebrate in style.

On the surface, such parties would seem counter to a Stoic way of life, so it may surprise you to learn that Seneca owned an incredible 300 tables, which he kept solely for the purpose of entertaining. These weren't just any old tables either. They were made of ivory, an expensive, luxurious item.

He wasn't the only ancient philosopher who enjoyed the finer things in life. Cato was fond of unwinding with a drink, as was Socrates. It's a pretty safe bet to assume Marcus Aurelius and Epictetus were the same.

So given that our view of Stoicism is one of a more ascetic lifestyle, how on earth can you square that with the fact that the Stoics loved their wine?

There's one little detail that explains it all. While we tend to drink our wine as it comes, the Greeks and Romans always diluted their wine with water. In fact, if you didn't, you would have been viewed as barbaric and someone with no self-discipline. The Roman poet Hesiod advised that the best way to savour your wine was to mix three parts water to one part of wine, something many of us would view as sacrilegious today, but to the Romans it was the other way round. Only an alcoholic would imbibe neat alcohol.

When we know the full picture, it fits perfectly with what a Stoic lifestyle should be. When you mix water with wine, you get a symbolic action representing one of the essential Stoic virtues: moderation. The Romans and Greeks made their wine strong, so it didn't take much for you to get drunk on it. So if you wanted to enjoy this simple pleasure to its fullest, it made sense to dilute it so the taste wasn't so strong and you could drink more of it without getting intoxicated.

It's an important metaphor for how you should be living a Stoic life. You can have whatever you want, but it's best taken in moderation. This way, you don't risk being seduced away from a virtuous path onto one that is solely about the pursuit of pleasure, diverting your focus away from what is under your control and instead placing it on chasing the next thrill, meaning you will never be satisfied.

Practical Exercises

✓ *Water down your vices.* Make a list of what vices, bad habits or indulgences you allow yourself to have. Think about the things you know your best self wouldn't do, but they're your weakness and possibly the only 'bad' thing you do, so you make allowances for that single thing.

I am not going to tell you that you have to give that thing up or, even worse, go cold turkey. Yes, we've discussed how you should embrace difficulties and make yourself undergo hardship to prepare yourself for the worst, but that doesn't mean you should deny yourself everything that makes you happy. (Now, if your vices are making you miserable, then your Stoic philosophy means you'll want to do something about that, but this is not the purpose of this particular exercise.)

Once you've written out your vice(s), think about a way in which you can water it down.

So, for example, if you like fizzy drinks, can you switch to diet or even flavoured fizzy water? If you like sugar in your tea or coffee, trying halving the amount you use and gradually cutting back. If you love to unwind in front of the television, alternate evenings watching with reading a good book. You could start by reading the works of the ancient Stoics to give you further inspiration. If you go out for a big night with your friends, alternate your alcoholic drinks with non-alcoholic ones. If you enjoy going to the movies with your partner, try going by yourself on occasion.

You can also apply this to the things you do that are good for you. If you spend every day at the gym, give yourself a rest day or try doing a gentler exercise like yoga or swimming on alternate days. If you work long hours, put some boundaries in place for yourself so that you will finish by a certain time and won't work any longer, or make sure you have a full day off at the weekend without getting caught up in chores and other types of work.

Summary

Moderation in everything is key. Dilute your vices and virtues for a more balanced life that enables you to appreciate everything for what it is.

- Recognise your vices and virtues and find ways to dilute them.

CHAPTER FOURTEEN

BE YOUR BEST SELF

"How easily dazzled and deceived we are by eloquence, job title, degrees, high honours, fancy possessions, expensive clothing, or a suave demeanour. Don't make the mistake of assuming celebrities, public figures, political leaders, the wealthy, or people with intellectual or artistic gifts are necessarily happy… Stop aspiring to be anyone but your own best self: for that does fall within your control."

—Epictetus

As if you haven't already seen just how advanced the Stoics were in their thinking, another aspect of their philosophy that deserves examination is their focus on what we would now term 'soft skills.' Unlike the skills we need to do our job, these are the traits that enable us to facilitate a supportive, productive working environment. As Marcus Aurelius puts it, "These are the characteristics of the rational soul: self-awareness, self-examination, and self-determination. It reaps its own harvest… It succeeds in its own purpose…"

If you have been following the exercises given in this book, you should already have a stronger understanding of how you interact with others. You should have been paying attention to your behaviour and how you react when things don't go your way, which will give you a sense of your strengths and weaknesses. While it can be hard to admit to our flaws and examine them for ways in which we can improve, to a Stoic, this is a source of joy. While others may try to keep up with the Joneses in a vain attempt to chase happiness, the Stoic looks at improving themselves rather than their material possessions, a pursuit that brings its own delight and reward.

Heraclitus was a philosopher who had a huge influence on the Stoics. He wrote that "self-deception [is] an awful disease and eyesight a lying sense." With the best will in the world, we can still be blind to our faults and fail to understand our contribution to our life experience. We tend to default to our comfort zone and learned behaviours, justifying our actions to ourselves that this is what's worked for us in the past so is clearly the best way forward.

But if what you've been doing in the past really was working for you, you wouldn't be reading this book, would you?

The Stoics had a very simple, two-step process for developing self-awareness. The first was to be suspicious about your perception and opinion about the people and events you encounter until you've tested them; the second was to take the opposite approach when it comes to evaluating other people's behaviour, by being sympathetic to their plight rather than automatically suspicious of their motives.

Epictetus advises us to take time out before reacting negatively, a little like counting to ten so you don't respond with the full force of your anger when something annoys you. He wrote, "First off, don't let the force of the impression carry you away. Say to it, 'hold up a bit and let me see who you are and where you are from – let me put you to the test.'"

Initially, it can seem difficult to always wait before reacting. In the real world, we don't always have time to breathe before we deal with a situation. But the more we do this, the easier it becomes.

Epictetus repeatedly used a word to reference this process: '*dokimazo.*' This means to test in the sense of someone checking to see whether a gold coin is pure gold or a gem is real. When we take a beat to test the situation and understand what is actually happening without peering through the fog of our preconception, we become better and better at it until we're able to instinctively understand the nuance of a situation and determine the best course to navigate through.

I'll say it again: *the only thing we can control is ourselves.* So it behoves you to act as compassionately and without judgement as possible while giving the other person the benefit of the doubt.

Marcus Aurelius advised, "Whenever you take offense at someone's wrongdoing, immediately turn to your own similar failings, such as seeing money as good, or pleasure, or a little fame – whatever form it takes. By thinking on this, you'll quickly forget your anger, considering also what compels them – for what else could they do? Or, if you are able, remove their compulsion."

If you are a leader in your field, or aspire to be, this is particularly important. People in positions of power are notorious for allowing that power to corrupt them. I'm sure you can think of a manager you've worked with who demotivated you and made it difficult for you to want to do your best. Yet Aurelius, one of the most powerful Roman emperors to have ever lived, was known for his compassion and humanity towards those around him.

As a Stoic, Aurelius believed we're all apprentices of life, constantly learning and never able to say we've conquered it because there are always more challenges to come. All we can do is our best, even when it seems that others have got it in for us.

He used wrestling as a metaphor to illustrate this point: "When your sparring partner scratches or head-butts you, you don't then make a show of it, or protest, or view him with suspicion or as plotting against you. And yet you keep an eye on him, not as an enemy or with suspicion, but with a healthy avoidance... You should act this way with all things in life. We should give a pass to many things with our fellow trainees. For, as I've said, it's possible to avoid without suspicion or hate."

If you can view life as a game and the people around you as your fellow competitors, with happiness as the prize, it becomes easier to make allowances for other people's weaknesses.

This ancient attitude has found its way into modern psychology. The notion of emotional intelligence arose from the methods of being suspicious of our own assumptions and judgments and having sympathy towards what someone else might be going through and trying to see things from their perspective instead of your own.

This is a lifelong practice and builds upon what we discussed in the chapter about taking the view from above. When you take Plato's view, you look at everything going on in the world – births, deaths, marriages, divorces, war, peace, crime, punishment, all possible combinations of the human experience balanced by their opposite and all containing a lesson and a striving towards balance.

This ebb and flow of polar opposites frequently causes us stress and friction, yet this is the natural way of the world and something we should welcome. All these events offer us the chance to engage with them to the fullest, learning more about ourselves and the world around us so we can be our most productive and happiest. They all give us the chance to be our very best self, no matter how challenging the current situation.

Seneca recommends that we should all "find our own Cato." This is someone you admire for the way they live their life and against whom we can measure up to become our best selves. Seneca said, "We can remove most sins if we have a witness standing by as we are about to go wrong. The soul should have someone it can respect, by whose example it can make its inner sanctum more inviolable."

Imagine your Cato is standing by your shoulder at all times. Would they approve of the way you're behaving or could they give you advice on how to improve?

This constant attention on how you can be your best self is at the heart of self-awareness and helps you develop your emotional intelligence. Over time, you'll find yourself become more even-tempered and self-controlled, able to work with others in a way that is just and harmonious and supports them to be the best they can be.

If you aspire to make the most of everything life has to offer by being your best self, you *need* your own Cato.

A common theme within Stoicism is to live according to nature, and this is something we've discussed a number of times throughout this book. This is particularly important as your Stoic practice develops and deepens, because we learn what is in our own nature and how we can nurture our desired traits and channel our more negative qualities in a positive direction.

As Seneca wrote, "Let us keep to the way which Nature has mapped out for us, and let us not swerve therefrom. If we follow Nature, all is easy and unobstructed; but if we combat Nature, our life differs not a whit from that of men who row against the current."

At first glance, this seems like a recipe for disaster. I mean, people are crude, selfish, mean, nasty… But while we may have learned behaviours and base impulses, the Nature the Stoics referred to was our gifts of logic and reason, our ability to rise above our instincts to act with care and deliberation.

This was best defined by Michel Dew, a modern Stoic scholar, who defined 'Human Nature' as "the condition of a human who is expressing the very best in his or her development, that is their ultimate 'best self'. They are growing and changing in an effort to reach the ultimate goal for a human being."

Thus, when you aspire to be yourself, you're not acting in a way that is unnatural for you. You are not trying to force yourself to be something you're not. You are, in fact, following the path that is your natural course and when you do what comes naturally, life becomes that much easier, regardless of the obstacles coming in your way. Indeed, to a Stoic, when you accept the limits and frustrations of your life and work with them rather than railing against them, that's when you are truly free.

As you continue on this journey towards self-awareness, you may well discover things about yourself you were previously unaware of. It may even be that you realise you're in the wrong career, for example, or there are things you should do that would bring you deep satisfaction but have not had the courage until now to pursue.

The more you learn about your innate inclinations and abilities, the more you can make the most of them to live a Stoically natural life. If you try to be something you're not, or attempt to do something for which you are not currently equipped, you'll make yourself miserable – and likely those around you too. But if you're living in harmony with your true self, you'll find you naturally gravitate towards where you're meant to be.

According to the Stoics, greed is not a natural desire, because it always drives us to want more and can never be satisfied. As such, if you allow yourself to be ruled by greed and continue to chase wealth, power and physical pleasures, you'll only be disappointed. You'll never be satisfied with what you have and can only ever be frustrated.

In any case, as Seneca puts it, wealth and poverty are all relative: "The man who restrains himself within the bounds set by nature will not notice poverty; the man who exceeds these bounds will be pursued by poverty, however rich he is."

In the first chapter of this book, you were advised to seek out misfortune. This is because you could lose everything at any given moment, so if you are prepared for it, you are more likely to have the fortitude to withstand the loss. When you stop constantly chasing an elusive definition of happiness and simply focus on yourself, you achieve a balance and contentment that are priceless.

As part of your quest to be your best self, you should approach your mundane, daily life with the same intensity and focus as if you were training for a marathon or concert performance. To a Stoic, no activity is more important than another – they all deserve the same care and attention in order for you to be your best. Being your best self is a habit you can develop through practice and determination and one anyone can acquire.

Like Epictetus said, "Desire and aversion, though powerful, are but habits. And we can train ourselves to have better habits. Restrain the habit of being repelled by all those things that aren't within your control, and focus instead on combating things within your power that are not good for you."

One way in which you can develop good habits is assessing your weaknesses and doing the opposite. Perhaps you love going out every night and getting drunk. Switch the alcohol for non-alcoholic drinks for a while and see the difference it makes. Maybe you have an irrational fear of spiders. Look into how you can overcome this so that while you may never love the creatures, you can tolerate them – you may even end up keeping one as a pet. They're surprisingly easy to care for!

Stoics placed a high emphasis on the truth and there's nothing more important than being honest with yourself. When you kid yourself about something, like staying in a relationship that is making you miserable or working in a job you hate, you become disconnected from your natural self and lose your way. A Stoic is brutally honest with themselves and others (although they are tactful in how they express that truth to those around them, being mindful of other people's circumstances.)

Epictetus advised you to "see things for what they really are, thereby sparing yourself the pain of false attachments and avoidable devastation." After all, it doesn't matter how we perceive something. Our perception doesn't change reality, so it is better for us to be honest with ourselves about the world about us and take Plato's view at all times. Instead of avoiding things that make us feel uncomfortable, actively examine those events causing us pain. When you face up to the reality of loss and disappointment, you break free from the chains of illusion and make it easier for yourself to be your best and stay alert at all times to ensure your motives and actions are in line with your nature.

It can be difficult to maintain this honesty with ourselves, particularly when we know tough times are on their way. But sticking your head in the sand and pretending everything will be fine will not help anyone and stunts your spiritual and emotional growth. Your best self knows how to weather the storm because it understands that this is temporary, as is everything else you experience in life.

Remember when we examined *amor fati* and how to turn obstacles into opportunities. Everything in life is an opportunity to be your best self. The onus is on you to rise to the challenge at all times. As Marcus Aurelius said,

"Loss is nothing else but change, and change is Nature's delight."

Death is the ultimate loss and the one thing many of struggle to deal with, even if we have a resilient attitude to everything else we've experienced. But Seneca told us we should not fear death, because "if you regard your last day not as a punishment but as a law of nature, the breast from which you have banished the dread of death no fear will dare to enter."

Death is the ultimate motivating force for us to be our best selves, because if we can truly say on our death bed that we always did our best, death holds no power over us.

The entire process of being our best arises from following our inner nature, and the cycle of life is part of that natural process. If you become in tune with your nature, it is easy to always choose the action or thought that is in accordance with your best self, whilst recognising that this is an ongoing process and a journey with no final destination beyond death.

You excel by knowing your personal limits and paying attention to only what's in your control. Following a Stoic philosophy in every waking moment of your life means you have a constant commitment to seeking the truth in reality and acting with kindness and respect as part of your responsibility to society at large. Accept death as a natural part of life and know that every new day is a gift you should be grateful for.

This is how you become your best self and fulfil your potential.

Practical Exercises

➤ *Change your perception.* Think about an argument or disagreement you've recently been involved in. In your journal, create a mind map of the situation. First, look at your own motives and actions. Try and be as objective as possible, as if you were discussing someone else. What did you do wrong? What could you have done differently? Why do you think you behaved in the way you did? What other explanations might there be for your behaviour? What would a Stoic approach have looked like?

Next, look at the motives and actions of the other person. What are the possible explanations for why they did what they did? What might be a factor for them that you are unaware of? What might be going on in their life that impacted their reactions to you?

When you are finished, choose the kindest explanation you can come with for the other party's behaviour and the harshest explanation for your own.

How does this change your understanding of the situation?

What will you do differently when something similar occurs in the future?

➤ *Find your own Cato.* In your journal, write a description of someone you know whom you admire and hold in high esteem. Why do you feel that way about them? What do they do that makes them worthy of your respect? What is it about their behaviour you would like to emulate?

Now detail what your best self looks like. Work with the person you are and don't include qualities you feel 'ought' to be there because other people will like them. Who are you now and what would the best version of that look like? Are you successful? What does that success look like? Are you wealthy or content with just having enough to pay the bills? How do you treat other people? What would your life be like if you were always this best version of yourself?

Now think about a situation recently that you found difficult to handle. How would your best self have reacted? How might things have been different if your best self was in that situation?

Every day for a week, write in your journal in the evening. First, detail what happened and then write it as if your best self had experienced that day. How would it have changed your day?

Repeat this exercise until you only have to write one version of the day because you have been at your best at all times.

➢ *Actively oppose your flaws.* Make a list of all your weaknesses, bad habits and undesirable traits. Choose one and come up with a way in which you can do the opposite to replace your negative tendencies with a more positive action. Maybe you love chocolate. Find an alternative healthy food you can snack on. Perhaps you're always late. Set your alarms ten minutes early and your clocks ten minutes fast to help you get ahead of yourself and arrive on time.

Whatever you choose, think about what your best self would do and train yourself in that habit.

Summary

Aim to be your best self at all times and work on developing positive habits in accordance with your true nature.

- Change your perception by examining a recent situation from all angles.
- Find your own Cato to help you make choices in accordance with your best self.
- Plan out a strategy to help you actively correct bad habits and negative thinking.

CHAPTER FIFTEEN

FINAL THOUGHTS

"That's why the philosophers warn us not to be satisfied with mere learning, but to add practice and then training. For as time passes we forget what we learned and end up doing the opposite, and hold opinions the opposite of what we should."
—Epictetus

After reading this book, you might be wondering where to start because there's so much there to do to be truly Stoic, but it is important to remember that Stoicism is a practical philosophy. It is meant to be learned through living. If you pick just one exercise that resonates with you and start with that one, you are already on your way.

You do not have to do everything at once. Even if you only take tiny steps, you will eventually reach your destination. This isn't a race. The more you work towards a

Stoic way of being, the easier it becomes and you won't worry about whether you can get it all done. You'll simply do it.

Two words are important here: '*Summum Bonum.*' It's a phrase first coined by Cicero and it translates to 'the highest good.' Whatever exercises you choose to do, they should be done with the highest good in mind, which, to the Stoics, meant virtue. Everything that happens to you is an opportunity for you to practice virtue in your response. No matter how painful, frightening or difficult the situation, if you react with virtue, the Stoics believed that the inevitable outcome would be all those things that are so important to us – happiness, fulfilment, success, honour, love, reputation.

In Cicero's words, "The man who has virtue is in need of nothing whatever for the purpose of living well."

According to the Stoics, there were only four virtues that someone should be ruled by: wisdom, courage, justice and temperance. If you allow your thoughts and actions to be determined by these four principles, you cannot go wrong.

Let's examine each of these virtues in more depth, starting with wisdom. The Stoics defined wisdom as the ability to determine what is good, what is evil and what is neither, what things to avoid and what would make no difference to your life of virtue, as well as being able to choose the right course.

Some things matter; a lot of things don't. A Stoic has the wisdom to determine which is which.

Or, as Epictetus put it, "Where then do I look for good and evil? Not to uncontrollable externals, but within myself to the choices that are my own." Between action and your reaction, there is a moment and it is in that moment you have the ability to decide how to respond. That moment is your opportunity to take everything you have learned and put it into practice or forget it all and allow yourself to be ruled by your irrational impulse.

Ultimately, how wise you are comes down to one thing, according to Seneca: "Works not words."

The next Stoic virtue was courage. In Epictetus' *Discourses,* he describes life as being "like a military campaign." By this, he meant we should always be on our guard for symbolic enemies that could disrupt your life. "One must serve on watch, another in reconnaissance, another on the front line… So it is for us—each person's life is a kind of battle, and a long and varied one too."

We all have an important role to play in our own personal battlefield of life. It's a very Stoic way of viewing things. Ultimately, nobody wins at life. We all eventually fall. Yet, despite the fact that death is inevitable, a Stoic continues to fight bravely to be virtuous at all times and not be corrupted by the countless temptations that continually bombard us.

One of the last things Seneca said was that "Nero can kill me, but he cannot harm me." Following a failed plot to overthrow the tyrannical emperor, Nero ordered the deaths of many leading figures, including his adviser, Seneca. While it is unlikely Seneca had anything to do with the plot, Nero was insistent that Seneca should kill himself, so the philosopher did as his ruler commanded.

His death was not easy and he took a long time to carry out Nero's orders, but Seneca died according to the philosophy he'd followed through life, knowing that this was merely another experience to be embraced.

This is an important notion to bear in mind when you are faced with your worst nightmares. You have the ability to stand up and do what's right, even if it costs you your life, because if you do, you cannot be harmed. This requires a lot of courage, particularly if you're going against social norms or the expectations of your loved ones. It takes grit and determination to stand up for what you believe in, but that's the Stoic way.

Even if you do not face the extreme situation Seneca was forced into, do not underestimate the daily battles we all have to deal with. Indeed, if you cannot recognise the conflict around you, the chances are high you need to work more on your self-awareness. When you start to follow a Stoic philosophy, you'll be in conflict with your former self, which will resist change and fight against your desire to improve yourself. You'll have to battle yourself when you go to bed and realise you haven't journaled that day, so you'll need to get up again to write down your thoughts. You'll have to battle against your natural inclination to yell insults at someone who pulls out in front of you in traffic. You'll have to battle against your desire to see an unpleasant colleague get in trouble when they ask you for help that you would rather not give.

Stoic courage goes beyond the obvious. It is that courage that drives everything we do.

You demonstrated courage when you decided to follow a Stoic philosophy. Now you need to continue to be brave as you continue down this path.

The third Stoic virtue is justice, which Marcus Aurelius viewed as the most important and "source of all the other virtues," and Cicero described as "the crowning glory of the virtues." After all, you can be brave but use that bravery to do stupid, dangerous things. You can be try to be wise but fail to take in the big picture.

Just as with the other virtues, the Stoic interpretation of justice goes beyond the superficial. Cicero examined this principle in great depth in his work *"De Officiis."* Translated as *"On Moral Duties,"* Cicero described justice in this text as the bond that holds society together and builds community.

He gave a number of points that were important to being just, which included never harming anyone and having respect for communal property because everyone needed to enjoy it while equally respecting private ownership. He said that none of us was born to be an individual alone; we are all here to treat each other well and follow our nature to act for the good of society as a whole.

Justice means always acting in good faith and being steadfast and true. Conversely, injustice is anything that injures or harms another. Cicero felt that the main reason people behaved in an unjust manner was because they were greedy and hurt others in order to get something they wanted. So, living in accordance with Stoic philosophy means that you should always strive to act with the good of the whole in mind, putting the needs of society before your own.

This doesn't mean you should martyr yourself for the sake of others' happiness. (Remember – focus only on that which you can control. You have no control over someone else's feelings.) However, a common thread throughout Stoic texts is the belief that everything is part of the whole, so as Marcus Aurelius puts it, "what injures the hive injures the bee."

Epictetus is even clearer. He wrote, "Seeking the very best in ourselves means actively caring for the welfare of other human beings." When you actively seek to do the right thing and avoid harming others, you become a just person.

Moving on to the notion of temperance, to a Stoic, this is all about finding that balance between overindulgence and asceticism, which will lead to a state of contented tranquillity. Finding that happy medium between chasing what you want and denying yourself pleasures will lead to misery. While it is important to experience times of deliberate hardship (as discussed in Chapter One), when you do this because you want to maintain an appearance of being a good person instead of simply experiencing it in the now, it's just as dangerous as giving in to temptation all the time.

Marcus Aurelius observed that "most of what we say and do is not essential. If you can eliminate it, you'll have more time, and more tranquillity. Ask yourself at every moment, 'Is this necessary?'"

If you have everything you need, you are truly rich, regardless of how much money you have in the bank. The only limit to wealth, according to Seneca, is "First, having what is essential, and second, having what is enough."

Stoics frequently referred to temperance as 'self-control' and they meant this on a holistic level. This self-control works on every level, from your ability to control your spending and consumerism, your ability to show compassion towards the people around you, even when they're behaving badly, and your ability to look for the opportunity in every obstacle and welcome it as a chance to learn and grow.

Strive for temperance and balance so you aren't relying on external things to make you happy or risk something bad happening, which can destroy your happiness.

That's it. Those four virtues are your key to a happy, fulfilling life. If it sounds simple, that's because it's meant to. The Stoics were all about breaking things down to their most basic form rather than dressing things up in complicated verbosity.

If you take only one thing away from this book, let it be the knowledge that you cannot control what happens around you, but you have full mastery of your response, and that response should be born out of courage, temperance, justice and wisdom. When you accept your lack of control, but know that your virtuous actions contribute to building a better world, it's a genuinely liberating feeling. It doesn't matter what happens; you *always* have the ability to do the right thing.

To finish, I'll leave you with this thought from Epictetus:

"Now is the time to get serious about living your ideals. How long can you afford to put off who you really want to be? Your nobler self cannot wait any longer. Put your principles into practice – now. Stop the excuses and the procrastination. This is your life! ... Decide to be extraordinary and do what you need to do – now."

He was right. You cannot afford to wait. You've only got a limited amount of time left on this earth.

So make the most of it. Start living like a Stoic and make the most of the gifts you were born with.

CPSIA information can be obtained
at www.ICGtesting.com
Printed in the USA
LVHW080327010321
680234LV00037B/593